Super-Cute Felt Animals

35 delightfully dainty projects to stitch

Laura Howard

CICO BOOKS
LONDON NEW YORK

Hello!

Published in 2013 by CICO Books
an imprint of Ryland Peters & Small Ltd
20–21 Jockey's Fields, London WC1R 4BW
519 Broadway, 5th Floor, New York, NY 10012

www.rylandpeters.com

10 9 8 7 6 5 4 3 2

A CIP catalogue record for this book is available from
the British Library.

ISBN: 978 1 78249 058 6

Printed in China

Editor: Emma Bastow
Designer: Louise Leffler
Photographer: Martin Norris
Illustrator: Stephen Dew

For digital editions, visit
www.cicobooks.com/apps.php

Acknowledgments

Huge thanks to Sheelagh and Chris
for all your support and the many
cups of tea! And big thanks to
everyone at Cico Books for all
your hard work in putting this
book together.

Contents

Introduction

Welcome to **Super-Cute Felt Animals**. With the tutorials in this book, a few supplies from your local craft store, and some basic sewing skills, you'll be making a whole menagerie of adorable animals in no time!

You'll find the templates for the animals at the back of the book. They're all shown at full size, so you can trace them and get stitching straight away, but if you prefer you can enlarge them to any size you like. Enlarging the designs slightly is also a great way to make them a bit easier to cut, sew, and stuff if you find the small projects a bit tricky.

The size of the animals makes them perfect for gift-giving as they're quick and easy to sew for birthdays and other occasions. All the animals would make sweet gifts as they are, but you can also adapt the patterns to make a wide range of keepsakes such as brooches, keyrings and mobiles (see pages 12-13).

I've also included suggestions throughout the book for how you can adapt the designs, which I hope will help spark your imagination!

Happy sewing,

Laura x

Materials

The primary material you are going to need is, of course, felt. There's a huge range of different felts available, but they can be divided into three main types.

Synthetic felt is the most widely available, and the type you'll probably find at your local craft store. The thickness and texture of this can vary depending on the range. You can also buy eco-friendly synthetic felt (made from recycled plastic), and patterned felt, which is printed with a pattern on the front and solid color on the back.

Felt made from 100 percent wool has a lovely soft texture, and it's usually slightly thicker than standard synthetic felt. It's a luxurious option, making it perfect for special projects, and it usually comes in a range of softer and more "natural" looking colors than most standard synthetic ranges.

Wool blend felt contains a blend of wool and synthetic fibers—between 30–70 percent wool depending on the range. It's cheaper and thinner than 100 percent wool felt, but has a similar soft texture and wide range of colors.

I used a mixture of synthetic and wool blend felts from different ranges to make the projects in this book. You can use any felt you like to make your animals as long as it's not too thick—$\frac{1}{16}$in (1-2mm) is ideal.

If you're adapting the projects to appliqué an animal on something that needs to be washable, make sure you choose a felt that you can wash! Some brands of synthetic felt are designed to be machine washable, but most felt should be gently hand washed. Felt tends to "pill" or "bobble" slightly when washed (especially with regular washing) and wool and wool blend felt will also shrink slightly and may not be colorfast. Check the packaging or with your supplier for washing instructions.

Two different types of thread are needed to make the projects: all-purpose sewing thread, and stranded cotton embroidery floss. Stranded floss is made up of six or eight strands, which are easily divisible so you can either sew with all the strands or separate the number you want. The more strands you use, the larger the needle you'll need to use.

Most of the projects involve using matching threads—this helps the stitching become "invisible" on the finished piece. Take a small scrap of your chosen felt colors with you when you go thread shopping so you can match the colors as closely as possible.

You will also need a bag of polyester toy stuffing/filling (also known as fiberfill), some black and white seed beads, and a selection of sequins. If you're using the suggestions in the Gift Ideas section (see pages 12–13) to adapt the patterns, you'll also need other craft supplies like ribbons, brooch clasps, and embroidery hoops.

Equipment

To make the designs in this book you will need: sewing scissors, ordinary scissors for cutting out the paper templates, pins, and needles (smaller ones for sewing thread, larger ones for embroidery floss). Some of the projects also require a pencil and a ruler or a bit of tracing paper, and you may want to use greaseproof paper or freezer paper, cellophane tape, or fabric pens to help you cut out your pattern pieces (see opposite for more details).

You will also need a pair of embroidery scissors. These have much smaller, narrower blades than standard sewing scissors so you can cut out small and intricate felt shapes with much more accuracy and control. You can buy cheap pairs from most craft stores, but if you're planning on doing a lot of felt crafting I'd recommend buying a quality pair with comfortable handles.

You'll also need a stuffing tool to help you stuff small shapes like the animals' legs. I actually use the closed blades of my embroidery scissors for this as they're great for poking into narrow shapes, but be very careful when using sharp scissors like this! You can use anything small and pointed—a pencil, a small crochet hook, orange sticks (found in manicure kits), or a narrow paintbrush with the bristles trimmed to $\frac{1}{4}$in (5mm) (the bristles will help grip the stuffing).

Alternatively, you can buy specially designed stuffing tools from many sewing shops. Specialist doll and toy-making shops may also sell small pairs of hemostats (surgical forceps) which are similar to scissors but blunt and designed for gripping, so they're ideal for adding small pieces of stuffing.

If you can't find any of the materials or equipment you need at your local craft store, check out the online stores listed on page 128.

Techniques

Cutting out felt shapes

There are four methods you can use to cut out your felt pieces: pinning or holding the paper templates, sticking pattern pieces in place with tape, making templates from freezer paper, or tracing the shapes directly onto the felt.

The simplest method is to pin the template in position or, if your template is too small to be pinned, just hold it in place between the thumb and forefinger of one hand while cutting around it with the other. Cut away any excess felt from around the template so you're working with a smaller piece of felt—this will make the felt much easier to maneuver—then use embroidery scissors to carefully cut out the shape, following the edge of the paper template and turning the felt slowly as you work your way around the template.

If you're using cellophane tape (or clear packing tape), cut a piece of tape just big enough to hold your paper template in position on the felt, and then cut around the template as normal. You need to use sharp scissors for this but don't use your best scissors as cutting through the tape will cause a sticky residue to build up and blunt the blades.

Freezer paper isn't widely available outside of the US but you may be able to find rolls or sheets of it in big craft stores or in specialist quilting stores. Trace or print your pattern pieces on the "paper" side, cut out the shapes, and place them shiny side down on your felt. Then use an iron (on a low heat with no steam) to iron the templates in place. The heat from the iron will cause the templates to stick temporarily to the felt so you can carefully cut around the shape and then peel the template off when you're done. The templates can be used several times before they will no longer stick. Always follow the instructions on your pack of freezer paper and be very careful when using your iron on synthetic or blended felt as the felt may melt!

Finally, you can trace around your paper pattern pieces directly onto the felt and then cut along the line. Most methods of drawing on the felt will leave a mark remaining when you've cut out the shape, so turn all your templates over before drawing around them so any marks will be on the back of your finished pieces. You can use an ordinary pen to mark your felt, or a specialist fabric pen like a quilter's chalk pen (for darker felt colors) or an air-erasable fabric marker (for lighter felt colors). The texture of some felt makes it difficult to draw a smooth line on, so trace around the pattern pieces slowly and always test the ink on a scrap piece of felt before you start.

Cutting out small shapes

When cutting out very small shapes without a template, start by cutting out a small square of felt, then cut out your shape from the square. To cut small circles, cut into the felt in a spiral motion, turning the felt around slowly as you cut (using your thumb as a pivot) and gradually making the spiral smaller until you get the size of circle you want.

I often cut two or three versions of a small shape before I get the one I'm happy with. Use leftover scraps of felt from other projects to practice cutting out the shape you want—tricky jobs like this always get easier with practice! If you're having difficulty cutting your small shapes accurately freehand, try drawing the shape you want onto a piece of paper, cutting it out, and then using a piece of clear tape to hold it onto the felt (as above).

Sewing

There are a few basic stitches that are used throughout the book.

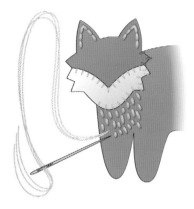

Whipstitch

To sew two layers of felt together along their edges, start stitching between the two layers, so the knot is hidden, passing the needle through to the front. Sew a stitch that overlaps the edge at a slight diagonal angle, passing the needle through the felt at the back, and sewing through both layers of felt at another slight angle through to the front, so the needle comes out a short distance along from where you started. Repeat this to sew up the whole edge.

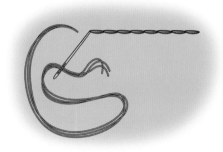

Backstitch

Start with one straight stitch, then pass the needle through the felt a stitch length away from the end of the stitch, as if you're starting a second straight stitch. Instead of moving "forward" along the line you're sewing, sew back toward the first stitch and pass the needle through the felt as close to the end of the first stitch as possible, so they form a continuous line. Repeat this, each time starting your stitches a stitch-length away from the previous stitch, and then sewing back to it.

Straight stitch

Pass the needle through to the front (pulling the thread completely through the felt), and then out the back again making one single stitch of the length required.

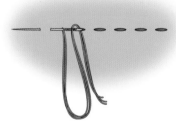

Running stitch

Pass the needle in and out in one step to create a row of even stitches, pulling the thread through the felt after each "in and out" (as pictured). Alternatively you can sew a line of small straight stitches (see above) to create the same effect. I usually do this when sewing through several layers of felt as I find it keeps my stitching neat.

To use whipstitch to sew one piece of felt onto another, start stitching at the back, passing the needle through to the front. Sew a stitch that overlaps the edge of the top piece of felt at a slight diagonal angle, and sew through the backing felt. Then sew back to the front at a slight angle, sewing through both layers, and repeat this until the top piece is sewn into position.

Sewing Tips

Sewing eyes or pupils

The animals in this book have either small black seed beads or a small black felt circles for their eyes or pupils. If you prefer (or if you find cutting out small felt circles tricky), you can stitch small black circles instead. To create a small dot for a pupil, cut a length of black embroidery floss (thread), separate half the strands (so for six-stranded floss, use three strands), and sew three or four very small straight stitches (see opposite) close together. To stitch a larger circle for an eye, separate black embroidery floss as before and sew a small star of four overlapping stitches, then sew about eight stitches of the same size on top to fill in the gaps between the stitches and create a circle.

Sewing the front and back of the animals together

When sewing the front and back pieces together, it's important to sew small and closely spaced whipstitches so there are no gaps in the stitching, which may allow stuffing to escape. Take extra care when sewing around tight curves and where two pieces of felt meet.

Sewing around the head of an animal

The final step of many of the projects is to sew a line of stitches around the head, pulling the layers together. As the whole animal is sewn together at this point, you can't start stitching on the "wrong" side of the felt (so the knot is hidden inside the finished animal) as you normally would. So, either ensure you finish the penultimate step with plenty of thread to spare, or start your final line of stitching by carefully pushing the needle into the seam a little away from where the stitched line will start, and then tug the thread gently as you pull the needle out so that the knot disappears into the seam.

Stuffing

Stuff the animals slowly, adding small pieces of stuffing bit by bit to gradually fill up the shape. It may surprise you at first just how little stuffing you need to add at a time, but you'll soon get the hang of the amount you need for different shapes.

Use a stuffing tool (see page 8) to poke tiny pieces into small shapes, like the animals' legs, and then use your finger(s) to stuff the bodies. Take your time—trying to stuff too quickly with large pieces of stuffing will result in a lumpy and uneven animal.

Add the stuffing gently, taking care not to push the stuffing through the seams. The more stuffing you add to a shape, the denser the stuffing will become as it compresses. The denser the stuffing, the firmer the finished piece will be and the more rounded the shape you're stuffing will become (if overstuffed, the shape can become distorted). You should aim to stuff the animals quite lightly, so a 3D shape is created but the animal remains light and squashable.

Push the stuffing away from the edge of the animal before you sew the final gap shut, so you can sew the seam shut without getting stuffing trapped in your stitching. When the edge is totally sewn shut, squash and squish the animal gently to even out the stuffing again. If you end up with a fiber or two of stuffing sticking out then poke them back into the seam if you can with your stuffing tool, or carefully trim or pull out the stray fibers.

Gift Ideas

All of the felt animals in this book would make perfect gifts just as they are, but for something different why not make larger versions or adapt the design in any of the following ways? To make larger felt animals, simply enlarge the templates at the back of the book. You may need to make some changes to adapt the designs slightly when you're making bigger versions—for example, adding more stitching or using more strands of embroidery floss than described; sewing on more sequins to cover a larger area; or cutting out a felt eye or pupil instead of using a seed bead. You will also need to start stuffing the animals sooner than described, so you can reach into all the corners of the shapes.

To make an ornament

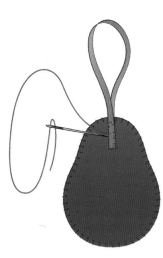

Adding a ribbon loop before sewing the front and back of the animal together will enable the animal to be hung. Cut a length of narrow ribbon and fold it over to make a loop, then sew the cut ends to the wrong side of the back body piece using whipstitch (see page 10) and matching sewing thread, sewing into the felt not through it. Continue following the instructions to sew the front and back of the animal together.

To make a garland

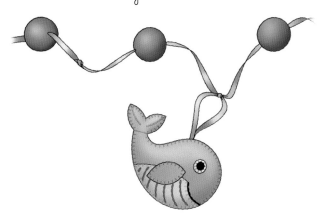

Sew ribbon loops onto a selection of felt animals, then string the animals onto a length of ribbon at regular intervals, knotting them in place and leaving a length of ribbon at each end to hang the garland. If you wish, add extra detail to the garland by stringing buttons or felt beads onto the ribbon in between the animals.

To make a keyring, bag charm, cellphone charm, or zipper charm

Use a small ribbon loop to attach a finding and turn the animals into keyrings, bag charms, or cellphone charms. The smaller felt animals (the baby animals or the Woodland Extras on page 30) would also make cute additions to the zippers on purses. Thread the ribbon through the keyring/zipper, etc., before sewing the ends into position as described above.

To make a mobile

Use invisible thread to suspend a selection of animals from either a store-bought mobile kit, two dowels or sticks tied together to form an X shape, or the inner circle of an embroidery hoop, then use yarn or thread to hang the mobile from a ceiling hook. You could use all the animals from one chapter to create a themed mobile, or mix and match your favorite designs from the book.

To make a brooch

Add a brooch clasp to the back felt shape before sewing the front and back of the animal together. Use a double thickness of sewing thread to sew the brooch clasp into position, sewing through each hole of the clasp several times to ensure a secure hold. Continue following the instructions to stuff and sew the front and back of your chosen animal together.

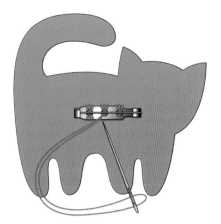

To make a flat brooch (rather than a stuffed one, as described on the left), appliqué an animal onto a piece of backing felt then carefully cut around the animal shape to create a border of felt around the edge. Use this shape as a template to cut out a second piece of felt. Turn the second piece over and sew on a brooch clasp, then turn it back over and sew the two shapes together with matching sewing thread. Use whipstitch (see page 10), or sew a line of running stitch (see page 10) flush with the edge of the animal so your stitching is hidden.

To appliqué the animals

Rather than creating a three-dimensional felt animal, simply sew the front of the animal and omit the stuffing to create a flat design, and then appliqué the animal onto anything you want to embellish—purses, lavender sachets, phone cozies or (if you enlarge the templates) bags or pillows. Look at the photo of the finished animal to work out which pieces you'll need to create the front of the animal only, and then use one of the following methods to sew the appliqué.

To make a "patch" to sew onto your chosen item, sew the front of the animal together, adding tails and feet, etc., to the back of this felt piece (instead of to the back piece as you would when making a stuffable animal). Sew the patch in position by whipstitching (see page 10) around the edge in matching sewing threads. This is ideal for adding an appliqué to a ready-made item, e.g. a store-bought purse.

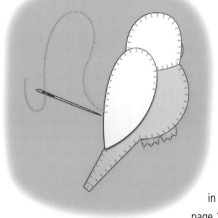

To sew the whole animal layer by layer onto backing felt or fabric, sew each piece in place with whipstitches (see page 10) to build up the design. Use the templates at the back of the book to add a cute animal to any project you're sewing, or just sew them onto a pretty piece of fabric stretched inside an embroidery hoop to create a piece of wall art—you could personalize this for a child's room by embroidering their name on the fabric below the animal.

Chapter one

In the Woods

The Fox Family

Meet a family of friendly foxes: a mama fox and two baby fox cubs. I used a bright orange felt for my foxes, but you could use red felt if you prefer. The fox cub templates provided are for the left-facing fox cub. To make the other cub just turn over all the pieces before you start sewing.

You will need:

Templates on page 112

Orange felt, approx. 6¾ x 7¼in (16.5 x 18cm)

White felt, approx. 2 x 2½in (5 x 6.5cm)

Small piece of black felt

Matching sewing threads

White embroidery floss (thread)

4 black seed beads, size 9/0

Polyester stuffing

Needles, scissors, pins

The Fox

1 Using the templates, cut out one head, one front body, and one back body from orange felt, and one tail, one face, and two eyes from white felt. Cut out two small circles for the pupils and an oval for the nose from black felt (see page 9 for tips on cutting out small shapes).

2 Position the head on the front body piece using the back body piece as a guide to ensure the front and back of the fox will line up neatly when sewn together. Whipstitch (see page 10) the head onto the front body using matching orange sewing thread.

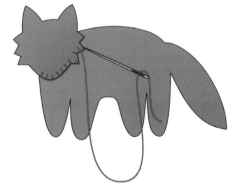

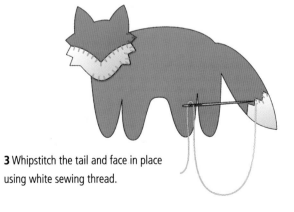

3 Whipstitch the tail and face in place using white sewing thread.

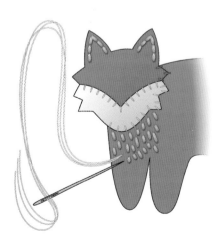

4 Cut a length of white embroidery floss and separate half the strands (so for six-stranded floss, use three strands). Switch to a larger needle if necessary and backstitch (see page 10) a line inside each of the fox's ears, then sew a series of small single stitches on the fox's chest.

5 Whipstitch the eyes, pupils, and nose to the head using matching sewing threads, then backstitch the fox's smile using black sewing thread.

6 Sew the front and back body pieces together at the tail using whipstitch in matching sewing threads, starting from where the tail meets the body and sewing down the bottom edge and back up along the top edge. Switch between orange and white sewing threads as required and stuff the tail gradually as you sew up the second side (see page 11 for tips on stuffing).

7 Whipstitch around the legs using matching orange sewing thread, starting just below the fox's head. Stuff the legs, then sew along the back and around the head, stuffing the fox gradually as you sew and switching to white sewing thread as you sew around the white section of the face.

8 If you wish, sew a line of running stitch (see page 10) flush around the edge of the fox's head from bottom to top using orange sewing thread to improve the shape. Carefully sew through all the layers of felt and stuffing to pull the layers closer together. Turn the fox back and forth as you sew to ensure the stitching is neat on both sides and finish neatly at the back.

The Cubs

1 Using the templates, for each cub cut out one head, one front body and one back body from orange felt, and one face from white felt. Cut out a small oval for the nose from black felt (see page 9 for tips on cutting out small shapes).

2 Position the head on the front body piece using the back body piece as a guide to ensure the front and back of the cub will line up neatly when sewn together. Whipstitch (see page 10) the head onto the front body using matching orange sewing thread.

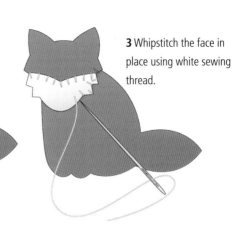

3 Whipstitch the face in place using white sewing thread.

4 Cut a length of white embroidery floss and separate half the strands (so for six-stranded floss, use three strands). Switch to a larger needle if necessary and backstitch (see page 10) a line inside each ear, then sew a series of small single stitches onto the cub's chest and tail.

5 Whipstitch the nose to the face using black sewing thread. Sew on two black seed beads for the eyes with three or four stitches of black sewing thread, then backstitch the cub's smile.

6 Backstitch lines onto the cub's body to mark out its legs, as pictured, using matching orange sewing thread.

7 Sew the front and back of the cub together using whipstitch in matching orange sewing thread, starting by sewing around the tail and then stuffing it (see page 11 for tips on stuffing). Sew up the body and around the head, switching to white sewing thread as necessary and then back to orange for the final section. Stuff the cub gradually as you sew, until the final gap has been sewn up.

8 If you wish, sew a line of running stitch around the bottom of the cub's head using matching orange sewing thread (see The Fox, step 8), finishing neatly at the back.

Wendy the Wise Owl

Hands up if you love owls! This owl is made using natural-colored felt, but you don't have to stick to brown. Add color with bright embroidery floss, or make the whole owl in your favorite colors. You could also add some sparkle by sewing sequins onto the owl's belly instead of embroidering it.

You will need:

Templates on page 113

Brown felt, approx. 3¼ x 4½in (8.5 x 11cm)

Light brown felt, approx. 3 x 3¾in (8 x 9.5cm)

Small pieces of orange, white, and black felt

Matching sewing threads

Brown and light brown embroidery floss (thread)

Polyester stuffing

Needles, scissors, pins

1 Using the templates, cut out four wings and one feather from brown felt, two bodies from light brown felt, two feet from orange felt, and two eyes from white felt. Cut out two small circles for the pupils from black felt (see page 9 for tips on cutting out small shapes).

Note: This owl has a single layer of felt for each foot, but to make the feet thicker or sturdier cut out four feet instead of two and sew the two layers together with running stitch (see page 10 or whipstitch (see page 10) in matching orange sewing thread. Or, if you find sewing two small pieces together a bit tricky, place the feet onto a scrap of matching felt and sew the layers together using small running stitches in matching sewing thread, following the outline of the feet and turning the felt back and forth as you sew to ensure the stitching is neat on both sides. Cut around the feet shapes to create two feet that are two layers thick.

2 Sew the head feather onto one of the body pieces as pictured using whipstitch (see page 10) in matching brown sewing thread along the bottom edge of the V.

3 Sew on the eyes, pupils, and beak using whipstitch in matching sewing threads. Cut a length of brown embroidery floss and separate half the strands (so for six-stranded floss, use three strands). Switch to a larger needle if necessary and sew irregular rows of vertical stitches across the owl's body for the feathers, varying the stitch length slightly and taking care not to pull too tightly and pucker the felt.

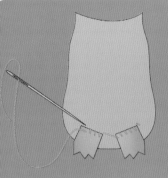

4 Sew the feet to the back body piece with a line of whipstitch in matching light brown sewing thread, sewing into the back piece of felt but not through it.

5 Cut a length of light brown embroidery floss and separate half the strands (so for six-stranded floss, use three strands). Switch to a larger needle if necessary and, starting at the top of the wing, sew a series of slightly curved lines in running stitch (see page 10) onto one left and one right wing shape, as pictured. Work down the wing and then back again, filling in the gaps to create a continuous line of stitching. Use the first wing as a guide for stitching the second to create two wings that are roughly a mirror image of each other.

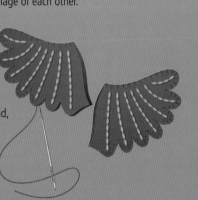

6 Whipstitch the two left wing shapes together using matching brown sewing thread, leaving the inside edge unstitched. Remove the pin, if you've used one, and repeat for the right wing shapes.

7 Sew the wings onto the back body piece using whipstitch in matching light brown sewing thread, sewing into the back piece of felt but not through it. You may find it helpful to place the front body piece on top of the wings to check how the finished owl will look before sewing the wings into their final position.

8 Sew the front and back body pieces together along the top of the head using small whipstitches in brown sewing thread matching the feather. Whipstitch around the edge of the owl using matching light brown sewing thread, starting at the bottom of one side and sewing up to the top. Turn the owl back and forth as you sew past the wings (and, later, the feet) to ensure the stitching is neat on both sides. Continue sewing down the other side, leaving a gap at the bottom large enough for your finger. Stuff the owl (see page 11 for tips on stuffing), sew-up the gap, and finish neatly at the back.

Sidney the Fluffy Squirrel

A fluffy squirrel looking for some acorns. The squirrel is very cute but is a bit tricky to stuff and sew together. I think he's well worth the effort, but I'd recommend trying some simpler projects first if you're new to sewing with felt.

You will need:

Templates on page 113

Gray felt, approx. 4½ x 8½in (11 x 21cm)

White felt, approx. 1¾ x 2½in (4.5 x 6.5cm)

Small pieces of light gray, dark gray, and black felt

Matching sewing threads

Polyester stuffing

Needle, scissors, pins

1 Using the templates, cut out one head, one front body, one back body, two tails, two legs, and one set of feet from gray felt, one belly and two eyes from white felt, one face from light gray felt, and one nose from dark gray felt. Cut out two small circles for the pupils from black felt (see page 9 for tips on cutting out small shapes).

Note: This squirrel has a single layer of felt for the feet, but to make the feet thicker or sturdier cut out an extra foot piece and sew the two layers together with running stitch (see page 10) or whipstitch (see page 10) in matching gray sewing thread. Or, if you find sewing two small pieces together a bit tricky, use the method for sewing the Owl's feet on page 20, sewing one shape onto a piece of felt and then cutting out the second layer after you've finished stitching.

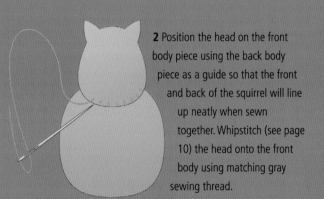

2 Position the head on the front body piece using the back body piece as a guide so that the front and back of the squirrel will line up neatly when sewn together. Whipstitch (see page 10) the head onto the front body using matching gray sewing thread.

3 Whipstitch the belly in position with gray thread, then whipstitch the face with matching thread.

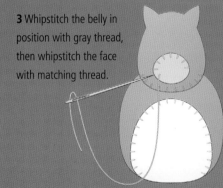

4 Whipstitch the arms to the body using matching gray sewing thread, then sew the nose, eyes, and pupils to the face using matching sewing threads.

5 Backstitch (see page 10) the squirrel's smile using black sewing thread, then sew six stitches to the face for the whiskers using dark gray thread. Set the front body piece aside.

6 Pin one of the tail shapes to the back body shape, as pictured. Turn the body and tail over, then sew a line of running stitch (see page 10) up the tail in matching gray sewing thread to join the two pieces together, taking care not to sew too close to the edge of the felt. Remove the pins.

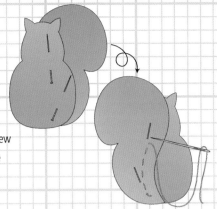

7 Whipstitch the feet to the back body piece using matching gray sewing thread, sewing into the back body piece but not through it.

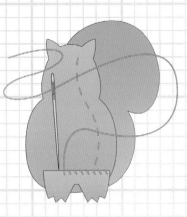

8 Backstitch a curved line onto the tail using matching gray sewing thread, as pictured, using small stitches to help create a natural-looking curve.

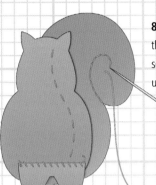

9 Place the two tail pieces together and whipstitch around the edge using matching gray sewing thread, starting at the top of the tail and sewing down the left-hand side. Stuff the tail lightly, stuffing gradually as you sew up the right hand side (see page 11 for tips on stuffing). Take care to only sew the two tail pieces together—fold the squirrel's body and feet out of the way of your stitching as necessary.

10 Sew the front and back of the squirrel together using whipstitch in matching gray sewing thread, starting where the tail meets the body on the right-hand side. Sew up to and around the head, taking care to only sew through the two layers of the body and not through the tail. Stuff the head and body gradually as you sew down the left side, then sew through all the layers of felt as you whipstitch along the bottom edge to join the body and tail together. Turn the squirrel back and forth as you sew past the feet to ensure the stitching is neat on both sides. Stuff gradually as you sew, until the final gap is sewn up.

11 If you wish, sew a line of running stitch flush around the bottom edge of the squirrel's head, from right to left, using matching gray sewing thread to improve the shape. (This can be a bit tricky as you've got to avoid sewing into the tail, so sew slowly and remember you can always pull out the stitches if you make a mistake!) Carefully sew through all the layers of felt and stuffing of the squirrel's body to pull the layers closer together. Turn the squirrel back and forth as you sew to ensure the stitching is neat on both sides, and to avoid sewing through the tail, finishing neatly at the back.

Ash the Adorable Badger

Say hello to this friendly badger! His stripy face is so distinctive—you could cut larger pieces for the face and make them into a cute little brooch. I've decorated my badger with black sequins, but if you'd like your badger's furry coat to be more gray than black you could add lots of single stitches using gray or metallic silver embroidery floss.

1 Using the templates, cut out two bodies, one nose, and one left and one right stripe from black felt and one head and two eyes from white felt. Cut out two small black felt circles for the pupils (see page 9 for tips on cutting out small shapes).

2 Whipstitch (see page 10) the left and right stripes onto the head as pictured, using black sewing thread. Whipstitch the eyes, pupils, and nose in position on the face in matching sewing thread. Backstitch (see page 10) a smile using black sewing thread.

You will need:

Templates on page 113

Black felt, approx. 4½ x 5¼in (11 x 13.5cm)

White felt, approx. 2 x 2in (5 x 5cm)

Matching sewing thread

White embroidery floss (thread)

Approx. 19 black sequins, ¼in (6mm) diameter

Polyester stuffing

Needles, scissors, pins

3 Cut a length of white embroidery floss and separate half the strands (so for six-stranded floss, use three strands). Switch to a larger needle if necessary and backstitch a curved line inside each of the badger's ears.

4 Position the head onto one of the body pieces and hold or pin in place. Whipstitch the head to the body using white sewing thread. Remove the pin, if you've used one.

5 Starting at the top, sew black sequins to the badger's back using three stitches in black sewing thread to secure each one, being careful not to sew the sequins too close to the edge of the felt.

6 Place the front and back body pieces together and hold or pin in place. Starting on the left side where the badger's head meets its body, whipstitch the front and back body pieces together around the legs and up toward the tail using black sewing thread. Stuff the legs (see page 11 for tips on stuffing).

7 Continue stitching around the badger, stuffing gradually as you go, using white sewing thread for the white sections of the head.

8 If you wish, stitch around the edge of the badger's head using running stitch (see page 10) in black sewing thread to improve the shape. Carefully sew through all the layers of felt and stuffing, to pull the layers closer together. Turn the badger back and forth as you sew to ensure the stitching is neat on both sides. Finish neatly at the back.

Betsy the Bashful Deer

Shh... this shy little deer is easily startled! She's made from light brown felt with pearlescent white seed beads for the spots on her back, but you could use a darker shade of brown felt and sew small stitches of white embroidery floss in place of the beads. If using a dark brown felt, you might like to sew the deer's smile using light brown sewing thread to help it stand out.

You will need:

Templates on page 114

Light brown felt, approx. 3¾ x 5¼in (9.5 x 13.5cm)

Small pieces of white and black felt

Matching sewing threads and dark brown thread

2 black seed beads, size 8/0

Approx. 7 white seed beads, size 8/0

Polyester stuffing

Needle, scissors, pins

1 Using the templates, cut out one front body piece, one back body piece, and one head piece from light brown felt, and two tail pieces from white felt. Cut out a small oval for the nose from black felt (see page 9 for tips on cutting out small shapes).

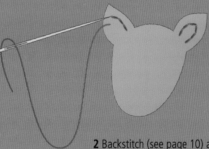

2 Backstitch (see page 10) a line around the inside of each ear as pictured, using dark brown sewing thread.

3 Sew the head onto the front body piece, lining up both sets of ears, using whipstitch (see page 10) in matching light brown sewing thread.

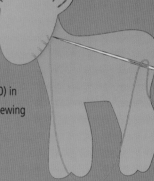

4 Sew the tail pieces onto the front and back body pieces as pictured, using whipstitch in white sewing thread, ensuring that the position of both tails matches so you'll be able to sew the front and back sections of the deer together later.

5 Sew two black seed beads onto the face for the eyes using three or four stitches of black sewing thread, then whipstitch the nose in position and backstitch the deer's smile. Sew white seed beads to the deer's back using three or four stitches of white sewing thread.

6 Sew the front and back body pieces together at the tail using whipstitch in white sewing thread. Starting from the left side where the head meets the body, whipstitch down and around the legs and up to just under the tail using matching light brown sewing thread. Lightly stuff the legs (see page 11 for tips on stuffing).

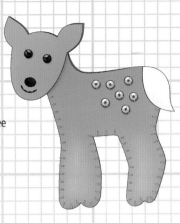

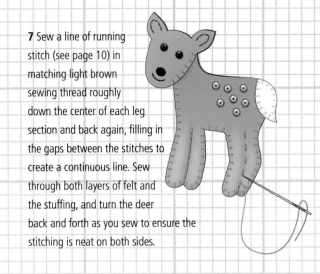

7 Sew a line of running stitch (see page 10) in matching light brown sewing thread roughly down the center of each leg section and back again, filling in the gaps between the stitches to create a continuous line. Sew through both layers of felt and the stuffing, and turn the deer back and forth as you sew to ensure the stitching is neat on both sides.

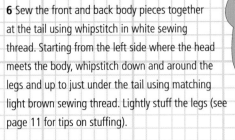

8 Whipstitch across the deer's back and around the head, stuffing gradually as you sew until the final gap is sewn shut. As you sew past each ear, whipstitch along the bottom (following the shape of the head) then up the right and down the left sides of the ear, turning the deer back and forth as you sew to ensure the stitching is neat on both sides.

9 If you wish, sew a line of running stitch flush around the edge of the deer's head from bottom to top using light brown sewing thread to improve the shape. Carefully sew through all the layers of felt and stuffing to pull the layers closer together. Turn the deer back and forth as you sew to ensure the stitching is neat on both sides and finish neatly at the back.

Harry the Happy Hedgehog

This little hedgehog is spiky but sweet! His spikes are embroidered using gold embroidery floss to give some extra sparkle. Pretty leaf-shaped sequins are great for the leaves that have stuck to him as he wanders through the undergrowth, but if you can't find some, simply cut some small leaf shapes from scraps of green felt.

You will need:

Templates on page 114

Dark brown felt, approx. 5¾ x 3in (14.5 x 8cm)

Light brown felt, approx. 3¼ x 4¾in (8.5 x 12cm)

Small pieces of white and black felt

Leaf-shaped sequins, or small leaves cut from scraps of green felt

Matching sewing threads

Metallic gold embroidery floss (thread)

Polyester stuffing

Needles, scissors, pins

Hello!

1 Using the templates, cut out two spikes from dark brown felt, two hedgehogs from light brown felt, and one eye from white felt. Also cut out a small oval for the pupil and a small circle for the nose from black felt (see page 9 for tips on cutting out small shapes).

2 Pin the hedgehog and spike pieces together as pictured, so the two hedgehogs are mirror images of each other. Using matching dark brown sewing thread, whipstitch (see page 10) the spike pieces in position and remove the pins. Set one of the hedgehogs aside.

3 Cut a length of gold embroidery floss and separate half the strands (so for six-stranded floss, use three strands). Switch to a larger needle if necessary and embroider V-shaped spikes over the dark brown felt of one of the hedgehogs, forming each V with two stitches and sewing the second stitch under the first where they meet (instead of next to it) to create a sharp point.

4 Sew the eye and pupil in position using whipstitch in matching sewing threads. Sew the nose in place with two very small black stitches in the center to form an X shape, then use a double-thickness of black sewing thread to backstitch (see page 10) the smile. To make a double-sided hedgehog, cut out the same pieces again and create a mirror-image face on the back of the hedgehog.

5 Arrange three leaf-shaped sequins or green felt leaf shapes on the hedgehog's back. If using sequins, secure with a few stitches of dark brown sewing thread. For felt leaves, either secure with a few stitches of green sewing thread at one end or sew a line of running stitch (see page 10) down the center of each leaf.

6 Hold the two hedgehog pieces together and whipstitch the edges of the light brown sections together using matching sewing thread, starting at the nose. For a double-sided hedgehog use black sewing thread to join the two noses together; for single-sided bend the nose forward to hold it out of the way as you sew past it.

7 Starting at the bottom of the hedgehog and then working around the spikes, whipstitch the edges of the dark brown sections together using matching dark brown thread, leaving a gap large enough for your finger. Stuff the hedgehog (see page 11 for tips on stuffing), whipstitch the gap closed, and finish neatly at the back.

Woodland Extras

A trio of things you'll find in the woods: a fir tree, a toadstool, and an acorn. You could make a whole set of toadstools using different bright colors for the caps, and lots of acorns with different colored stitching. If you don't have any ginger felt for the acorn, use brown instead or match the felt to the color of the stitching on the cap. The fir tree would make a great Christmas ornament, decorated with colorful sequins, seed beads, or embroidery.

You will need:

Templates on page 115

Green felt, approx. 3¼ x 6¾in (8.5 x 16.5cm)

Small pieces of brown and white felt

Red felt, approx. 1¾ x 2½in (4.5 x 6.5cm)

Light brown felt, approx. 1¾ x 2in (4.5 x 5cm)

Ginger felt, approx. 2 x 3in (5 x 8cm)

Matching sewing threads and black thread

Spring green and orange embroidery floss (thread)

Approx. 10 white seed beads, size 8/0

2 black seed beads, size 9/0

Polyester stuffing

Needles, scissors, pins

The Fir Tree

1 Using the templates, cut out one of each tree piece from green felt and two trunk pieces from brown felt.

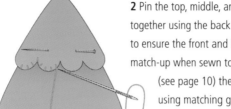

2 Pin the top, middle, and bottom tree pieces together using the back tree piece as a guide to ensure the front and back of the tree will match-up when sewn together. Whipstitch (see page 10) the three pieces together using matching green sewing thread, as pictured, and remove the pins.

3 Cut a length of spring green embroidery floss and separate half the strands (so for six-stranded floss, use three strands). Switch to a larger needle if necessary and cover the front of the tree with randomly-placed single stitches, taking care not to pull the stitches too tight and pucker the felt.

4 Whipstitch the two trunk pieces together using matching brown sewing thread, leaving the top edge open. Stuff the bottom half of the trunk (see page 11 for tips on stuffing).

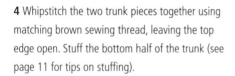

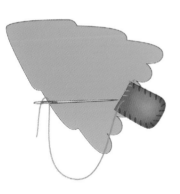

5 Whipstitch the trunk to the back tree piece using matching green sewing thread, sewing into the green felt but not through it.

6 Sew the front and back of the tree together using whipstitch in matching green sewing thread. Start from near the top as pictured, and turn the tree back and forth as you sew past the trunk to ensure the stitching is neat on both sides. Stuff the tree gradually as you sew up the second side, close up the final gap, and finish the stitching neatly at the back.

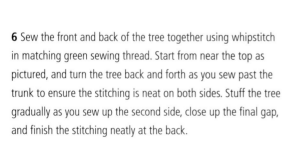

The Toadstool

1 Using the templates, cut out two caps from red felt and two stalks from white felt.

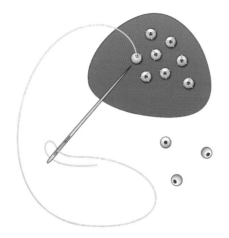

2 Sew white seed beads onto one of the cap pieces using three or four stitches of white sewing thread, taking care not to sew them too close to the edge of the felt.

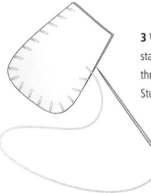

3 Whipstitch (see page 10) the two stalks together using white sewing thread, leaving the top edge open. Stuff the bottom two-thirds of the stalk (see page 11 for tips on stuffing).

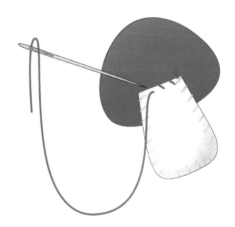

4 Whipstitch the stalk to the back cap piece using matching red sewing thread, sewing into the red felt but not through it.

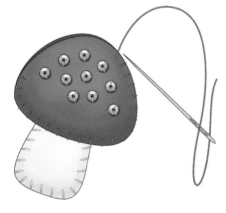

5 Sew the front and back of the cap together using whipstitch in matching red sewing thread, leaving a gap for stuffing. Turn the toadstool back and forth as you sew past the stalk to ensure the stitching is neat on both sides. Stuff the cap then whipstitch the final gap closed, finishing the stitching neatly at the back.

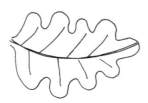

The Acorn

1 Using the templates, cut out two caps from light brown felt and two acorns from ginger felt.

2 Sew a cap to each acorn piece using whipstitch (see page 10) in matching light brown sewing thread, to create two acorns that are a mirror image of each other.

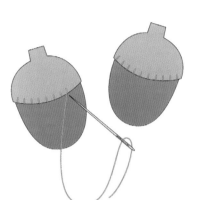

3 Cut a length of orange embroidery floss and separate half the strands (so for six-stranded floss, use three strands). Switch to a larger needle if necessary and backstitch (see page 10) a lattice pattern onto the front acorn cap by sewing a series of lines in one direction, and then sewing a second set crossing the first at a right angle. Take care not to stitch too close to the edge of the felt.

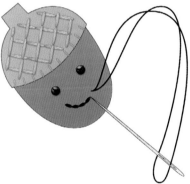

4 Sew two black seed beads onto the acorn for the eyes with three or four stitches of black sewing thread, then backstitch the acorn's smile using a double-thickness of black sewing thread.

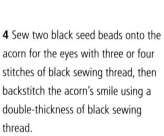

5 Sew the front and the back of the acorn together around the cap using whipstitch in matching light brown sewing thread.

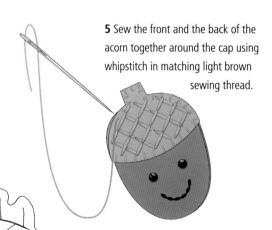

6 Whipstitch the rest of the acorn together using ginger sewing thread, leaving a small gap for stuffing. Stuff the acorn (see page 11 for tips on stuffing) and sew the final gap closed, finishing the stitching neatly at the back.

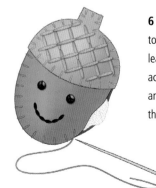

Chapter two
On Safari

The Elephant Family

A mama elephant and two calves—I know baby elephants aren't actually pink and blue but they do look very cute! Why not make a whole herd of elephants in different pretty colors? The baby elephants are constructed in a similar way to the big elephant, but the patterns are slightly different so make sure you refer to the notes when sewing the babies.

You will need:

Templates on page 116

Light gray felt, approx. 4½ x 6¾in (11 x 16cm)

Small pieces of black and white felt

Light blue felt, approx. 3¾ x 4in (9.5 x 10cm)

Light pink felt, approx. 3¾ x 4in (9.5 x 10cm)

Matching sewing threads and black thread

4 black seed beads, size 9/0

Polyester stuffing

Needle, scissors, pins

The Large Elephant

1 Using the templates, cut out one head, one set of ears, one front body, one back body, and one tail from light gray felt and two eyes from white felt. Cut out two small circles from black felt for the pupils (see page 9 for tips on cutting out small shapes).

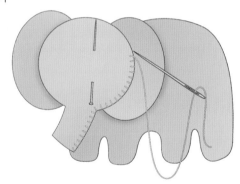

2 Pin the head and ears onto the front body piece, as pictured, ensuring the trunk lines up with the trunk outline on the back body piece (so the front and back of your elephant will match up when you sew them together later). Whipstitch (see page 10) together along the right side of the trunk and head using matching sewing thread. Remove the pin.

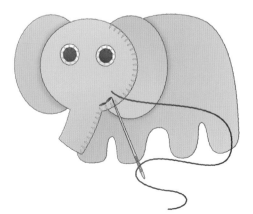

3 Whipstitch the eyes and pupils in position using matching sewing threads, then backstitch (see page 10) the elephant's smile using black sewing thread.

4 Place the tail onto a scrap piece of light gray felt. Starting at the top of the tail, sew a line of running stitch (see page 10) in matching thread to the bottom and back again, filling in the gaps between the stitches to create a continuous line, as pictured. Turn the felt back and forth as you sew to ensure the stitching is neat on both sides. Cut around the tail shape to create a tail that's two layers thick.

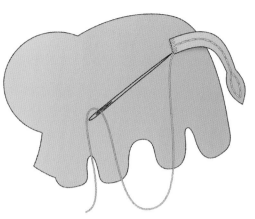

5 Sew the tail to the back body piece using whipstitches in matching sewing thread, sewing into the back piece of felt but not through it.

6 Sew the front and back body pieces together using whipstitches in matching sewing thread, starting at the front leg and sewing around all the legs and up toward the tail. Stuff the back three legs (see page 11 for tips on stuffing).

7 Sew along the back and around to where the head joins the body, folding the ear forward as you sew behind it. Stuff the elephant's body. Then sew from the bottom of the trunk around the top of the head, stuffing as you sew.

8 If you wish, sew a line of running stitch flush around the edge of the elephant's head and down the side of its trunk using matching sewing thread—this will improve the shape of the finished elephant. Carefully sew through all the layers of felt and stuffing to pull the layers closer together. Turn the elephant back and forth as you sew to ensure the stitching is neat on both sides, finishing neatly at the back.

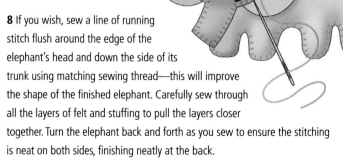

The Baby Elephants

1 Using the templates provided, for each baby elephant cut out one head, one set of ears, one front body, one back body, and one tail from light blue or light pink felt.

2 Follow step 2 of the Large Elephant instructions, but hold the pieces together carefully or baste (tack) them in place with a large stitch or two, which you can remove afterward, as the pieces are too small to easily pin together.

3 Continue to step 3, sewing two black seed beads onto the baby elephant's face instead of the felt eyes, securing each bead in place using a few stitches of black sewing thread.

4 Follow steps 4 and 5 of the Large Elephant instruction. Continue to step 6 but stuff all four legs instead of just three, then follow steps 7, 8, and 9.

Hello!

Chris the Cute Crocodile

Don't worry, this friendly crocodile doesn't bite! This is one of the easiest of my safari animals to sew—a great place to start if you're new to felting. I've decorated my crocodile with round sequins, but little star sequins would also look great.

You will need:

Templates on page 114

Green felt, approx. 4 x 5in (10 x 13cm)

Small pieces of white and black felt

Matching sewing threads

Green sequins, approx. ¼in (5mm) diameter

Polyester stuffing

Needle, scissors, pins

1 Using the templates, cut out two crocodiles from green felt and one eye from white felt. Also cut out a small black circle for the pupil (see page 9 for tips on cutting out small shapes).

2 Using whipstitch (see page 10) and matching thread, sew the eye and the pupil in position on one of the crocodile shapes, as pictured.

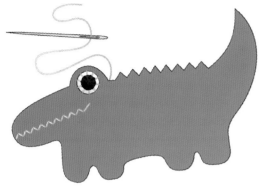

3 Starting at the tip of the snout, backstitch (see page 10) a zigzag line slanting upward in white sewing thread to form the crocodile's toothy mouth. Finish with a slightly longer upward stitch, as pictured.

4 Starting at the tail, sew green sequins to the crocodile's tail and back using three stitches of matching green sewing thread to secure each, taking care not to sew them too close to the edge of the felt.

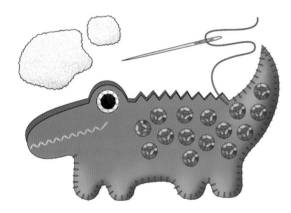

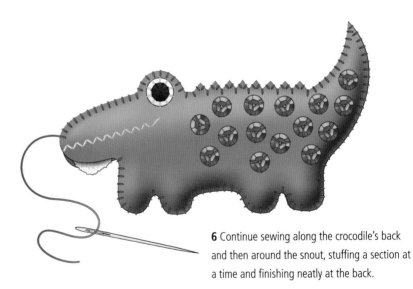

5 Hold or pin the two body pieces together. Starting from just under the crocodile's snout, sew the two pieces together around the legs using whipstitch in matching sewing thread. Remove the pin, if you've used one, and stuff the feet. Gradually sew around the tail, stuffing it bit by bit as you sew (see page 11 for tips on stuffing).

6 Continue sewing along the crocodile's back and then around the snout, stuffing a section at a time and finishing neatly at the back.

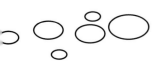

Leopold the Lazy Lion

Grrr! This lion is not very fierce, but he still likes to practice his roar! He would make a great gift for anyone you know who is the star sign Leo. This lion has an orange mane, but he would also look rather fetching with a brightly colored one—maybe a royal purple for the so-called "king of the jungle."

You will need:

Templates on page 115

Orange felt, approx. 2½ x 4¾in (6.5 x 12cm)

Gold or light orange felt, approx. 4½ x 4¾in (11 x 12cm)

Small pieces of white, black, and brown felt

Matching sewing threads

Light orange embroidery floss (thread)

Polyester stuffing

Needles, scissors, pins

1 Using the templates, cut out two bodies, two faces, and one tail from gold or light orange felt, two manes from orange felt, and two eyes from white felt. Cut out two small circles from black felt for the pupils, and a small nose from brown felt (see page 9 for tips on cutting out small shapes).

2 Pin the mane and body pieces together as pictured, so the two lions are a mirror image of each other. Stitch the manes in place using running stitch (see page 10) in matching orange sewing thread. Remove the pins and set one of the lions aside.

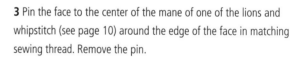

3 Pin the face to the center of the mane of one of the lions and whipstitch (see page 10) around the edge of the face in matching sewing thread. Remove the pin.

4 Stitch the eyes, pupils, and nose in position using whipstitch in matching sewing threads, then use a double-thickness of brown sewing thread to backstitch (see page 10) the smile. Finish the face by using a single thickness of brown sewing thread to embroider three stitches on either side of the nose to form the whiskers.

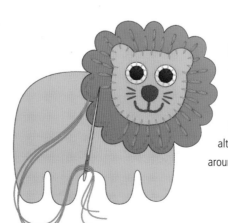

5 Cut a length of light orange embroidery floss and separate half the strands (so for six-stranded floss, use three strands). Switch to a larger needle if necessary and backstitch lines on the mane as pictured, sewing two stitches alternating with one stitch to form a starburst around the lion's face.

6 Place the tail onto a scrap piece of matching felt. Starting at the top of the tail, sew a line of running stitch in matching thread to the bottom and back again, filling in the gaps between the stitches to create a continuous line, as pictured. Turn the felt back and forth as you sew to ensure the stitching is neat on both sides. Cut around the tail shape to create a tail that's two layers thick.

7 Attach the tail on the "wrong" side of the back of the lion using whipstitches in matching sewing thread, sewing into the back piece of felt but not through it.

8 Sew the front and back body pieces together using whipstitches in matching sewing thread, starting where the mane meets the front leg and sewing around all the legs and up toward the tail. Stuff the legs (see page 11 for tips on stuffing) then sew past the tail and across the back, turning the lion back and forth as you sew past the tail to ensure the stitches are neat on both sides. Stuff the lion's body.

9 Whipstitch around the edge of the mane in matching orange sewing thread, leaving a gap big enough for your finger. Stuff the mane then whipstitch the gap closed, finishing neatly at the back.

Harriet the Smiling Hippo

This fat little hippo is very pleased to meet you! Like the crocodile on page 40, this hippo is quite easy to sew and stuff so it would make a good beginner-friendly project. Add some sparkle to your hippo if you want by adding lots of purple sequins to her body.

You will need:

Templates on page 117

Lilac felt, approx. 4½ x 4¾in (11 x 12cm)

Small pieces of white and black felt

Matching sewing threads and dark purple thread

Polyester stuffing

Needle, scissors, pins

1 Using the templates, cut out one head, one front body, and one back body from lilac felt and two eyes from white felt. Cut out two small black circles for the pupils (see page 9 for tips on cutting out small shapes).

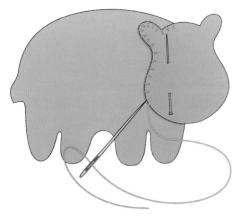

2 Position the head on the front body piece, using the back body piece as a guide so the front and back of the hippo will match up when you sew them together later. Pin or hold the two pieces together and whipstitch (see page 10) the head in place using matching lilac sewing thread. Remove the pin, if you've used one.

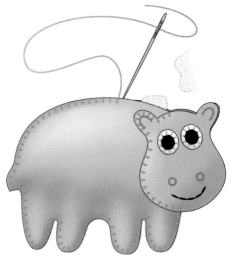

3 Sew the eyes and pupils onto the face using whipstitch in matching white and black sewing threads. Backstitch (see page 10) the hippo's smile using black sewing thread, then use dark purple sewing thread and very small stitches to backstitch a curved line onto each ear, and to embroider two small circles to form the nostrils.

4 Sew the front and back body pieces together using whipstitches in matching sewing thread, starting on the right where the hippo's head meets its body. Sew all the way along the bottom of the hippo and then stuff the legs (see page 11 for tips on stuffing).

5 Continue to whipstitch the edges of the hippo together, stuffing gradually until the final gap is closed.

6 If you wish, use matching lilac sewing thread to sew a line of running stitch flush around the edge of the hippo's head, sewing upward from the bottom of the head, to improve the shape. Carefully sew through all the layers of felt and stuffing to pull the layers closer together. Turn the hippo back and forth as you sew to ensure the stitching is neat on both sides, finishing neatly at the back.

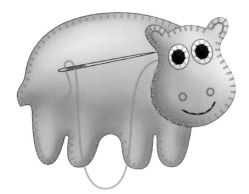

Gerald the Hungry Giraffe

A happy giraffe, taking a break from munching on some leaves. The legs are quite tricky to stuff, so make sure you take your time or enlarge the pattern slightly if you're not confident stuffing small shapes.

You will need:

Templates on page 116

Yellow felt, approx. 4½ x 6in (11 x 15cm)

Brown felt, approx. 2 x 3in (5 x 8cm)

Matching sewing threads and black thread

Gold sequins, approx. ¼in (6mm) diameter

2 black seed beads, size 8/0

Polyester stuffing

Needle, scissors, pins

1 Using the templates, cut out two giraffes and two ears from yellow felt and one mane and one tail from brown felt.

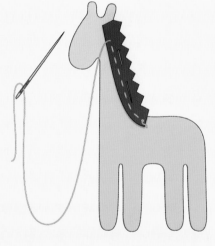

2 Position the mane on one of the giraffe shapes as pictured, and pin it in place. Check that all the triangular points of the mane can be seen poking out from the yellow felt when the two giraffe shapes are placed together, then sew the mane in position with a line of running stitch (see page 10) in matching yellow thread. Turn the giraffe back and forth as you sew to ensure the stitching is neat on both sides, then remove the pin.

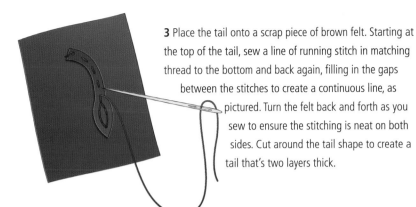

3 Place the tail onto a scrap piece of brown felt. Starting at the top of the tail, sew a line of running stitch in matching thread to the bottom and back again, filling in the gaps between the stitches to create a continuous line, as pictured. Turn the felt back and forth as you sew to ensure the stitching is neat on both sides. Cut around the tail shape to create a tail that's two layers thick.

4 Sew the tail to the body piece using whipstitches (see page 10) in matching sewing thread, sewing into the back piece of felt but not through it.

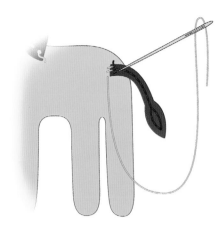

5 Sew one ear onto the back giraffe piece and one onto the front as pictured, using a few whipstitches along the bottom of each ear in matching yellow thread. You may find it helpful to place the two giraffe pieces on top of each other when positioning the ears so you can see how the head will look when the giraffe is finished. Set the back piece aside.

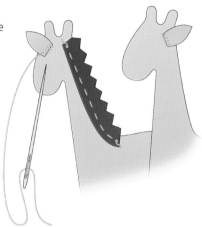

6 Sew two black seed beads on the face for the eyes using three or four stitches of black sewing thread, then use two strands of black thread to sew two short stitches for the nostrils and backstitch the giraffe's smile.

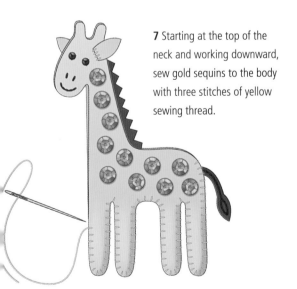

7 Starting at the top of the neck and working downward, sew gold sequins to the body with three stitches of yellow sewing thread.

8 Sew the front and back body pieces together using whipstitches in matching yellow thread, starting from the tail and sewing around the legs. Sew the legs gradually, about a third of each leg at a time, stuffing them bit by bit as you sew (see page 11 for tips on stuffing).

9 Whipstitch around the giraffe's body, up the neck, and around the horns. Turn the giraffe back and forth as you sew past the mane to ensure the stitching is neat on both sides, and fold the ear forward as you sew behind it. Stuff the body then gradually sew up the other side of the neck and around the head, stuffing bit by bit as you sew and finishing neatly at the back.

Sophie the Sweet Zebra

A very stripy zebra! Make sure you use white felt that's not too thin or soft so it will support the embroidery, and so the zebra shape won't be distorted as you stitch the stripes. If you wish, you could sew your zebra's stripes in a bright color, or use five or six different shades of floss to make a rainbow zebra.

You will need:

Templates on page 117

Black felt, approx. 2 x 3¾in (5 x 9.5cm)

White felt, approx. 3¾ x 5¾in (9.5 x 14.5cm)

Matching sewing threads

Black embroidery floss (thread)

Polyester stuffing

Needles, scissors, pins

1 Using the templates, cut out one mane, one tail, and one muzzle from black felt and two zebras, two ears, and one eye from white felt. Cut out a small circle from black felt for the pupil (see page 9 for tips on cutting out small shapes).

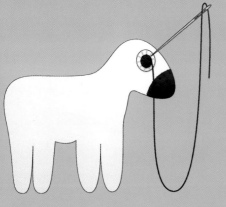

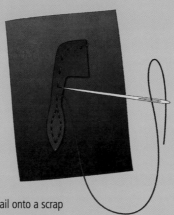

2 Whipstitch (see page 10) the muzzle, eye and pupil onto one of the zebra pieces using matching sewing threads.

3 Place the tail onto a scrap piece of black felt. Starting at the top of the tail, sew a line of running stitch (see page 10) in matching thread to the bottom and back again, filling in the gaps between the stitches to create a continuous line, as pictured. Turn the felt back and forth as you sew to ensure the stitching is neat on both sides. Cut around the tail shape to create a tail that's two layers thick.

4 Sew the tail onto the back zebra piece using whipstitches in white sewing thread, sewing into the white felt but not through it. Pin the mane to the zebra's neck as pictured, then turn the zebra over to check that enough of the mane will be visible when the front and back of the zebra are sewn together. Adjust as necessary then whipstitch the mane in place using white sewing thread. Remove the pin.

5 Sew an ear onto each of the zebra pieces, as pictured, using a few whipstitches in white sewing thread at the bottom of each ear.

6 Backstitch (see page 10) a line around the inside of the ear and around the eye on the front of the zebra using black sewing thread, then switch to white sewing thread and backstitch a circle of small stitches for each nostril and a curved line of three stitches for the smile.

7 Cut a length of black embroidery floss and separate half the strands (so for six-stranded floss, use three strands). Switch to a larger needle if necessary and backstitch a series of irregular stripes along the zebra's head, neck, and back, as pictured. Start at the zebra's muzzle and work backward, taking care not to pull the stitches too tight and pucker the felt.

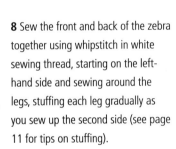

8 Sew the front and back of the zebra together using whipstitch in white sewing thread, starting on the left-hand side and sewing around the legs, stuffing each leg gradually as you sew up the second side (see page 11 for tips on stuffing).

9 Whipstitch up to and around the head, switching to black thread as you sew around the muzzle then back to white thread. Turn the zebra back and forth as you sew past the mane and tail to ensure the stitching is neat on both sides, and take care not to sew across the black lines as you sew past the front ear. Stuff the zebra's head, neck, and body gradually as you sew until the final gap has been sewn up, finishing neatly at the back.

Chapter three

Under the Sea

The Fish Family

Say hello to a whole shoal of sparkly fish—a big fish and lots of little fry (a.k.a. baby fish!). I used turquoise and lilac felt for my family of fish, with lots of shiny silver sequins to create the effect of scales. You could use any two colors you fancy, or maybe use a whole assortment of felt colors and sequins to make some rainbow fish!

You will need:

Templates on page 118

Turquoise felt, approx. 5¼ x 7¼in (13.5 x 18cm)

Small pieces of white and black felt

Lilac felt, approx. 4 x 4¾ in (10 x 12cm)

Matching sewing threads and black thread

Lilac embroidery floss (thread)

Silver sequins, ¼in (6mm) in diameter

4 black seed beads, size 9/0

Polyester stuffing

Needles, scissors, pins

The Large Fish

1 Using the templates, cut out two fish shapes and one of each of the fin shapes from turquoise felt, one eye from the white felt, and three large scale pieces and one small scale piece from lilac felt. Cut out a small black oval for the pupil from the black felt (see page 9 for tips on cutting out small shapes).

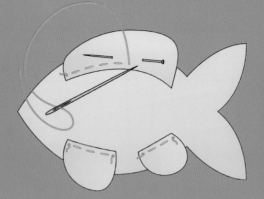

2 To make the back of the fish, hold or pin the three fins on one of the fish pieces as pictured, and sew them in place using running stitch (see page 10) in matching sewing thread. Remove the pins and set aside.

3 Cut a length of lilac embroidery floss and separate half the strands (so for six-stranded floss, use three strands). Switch to a larger needle if necessary and use backstitch (see page 10) to embroider a line around the edge and down the center of each tail fin of the second fish piece, as pictured. Take care not to pull too tight and pucker the felt.

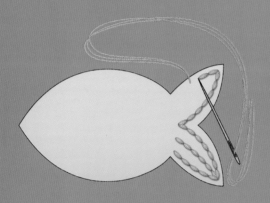

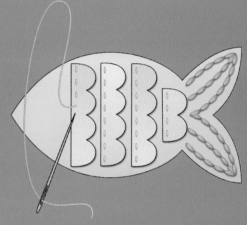

4 Starting at the tail-end of the fish attach the four lilac scale pieces by sewing a line of running stitch along each straight edge using matching sewing thread. Hold each one in position as you sew and leave a very small space between each row.

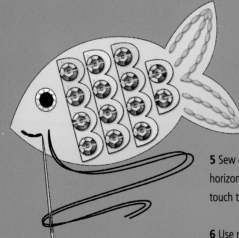

5 Sew one sequin onto each scallop of the felt scales using two horizontal stitches in lilac sewing thread. Position the sequins so they touch the straight edge of the felt scales.

6 Use matching sewing thread to whipstitch (see page 10) the eye and pupil into position, then use a double thickness of black thread to backstitch the smile.

7 Place the front and back of the fish together and sew around the edge of the tail using running stitch in matching sewing thread. Sew a vertical line between the tail and the body so that the tail will stay flat when the fish is stuffed.

8 Whipstitch the fish's body together using matching sewing thread, turning the fish back and forth when you sew past the fins to ensure the stitching is neat on both sides. Leave a gap large enough for your finger and stuff the fish (see page 11 for tips on stuffing). Whipstitch the gap closed and finish neatly at the back.

The Baby Fish

1 Using the templates, for each baby fish cut out two baby fish shapes from turquoise or lilac felt.

2 Starting at the tail-end, sew three rows of sequins onto one of the baby fish pieces using two horizontal stitches in matching sewing thread. Position the sequins as close together as possible but not too close to the edge of the felt as you'll need to sew around them later.

3 Sew a black seed bead eye onto the baby fish using three or four stitches of black sewing thread and use tiny stitches to backstitch (see page 10) a smile.

4 To join the front and back pieces of the baby fish, hold the pieces together and start by sewing a line of running stitch (see page 10) around the edge of the tail using matching sewing thread. Sew a vertical line between the tail and the main body, then whipstitch (see page 10) almost all the way around the body of the fish, leaving a small gap. Stuff the fish (see page 11 for tips on stuffing), whipstitch the gap closed, and finish neatly at the back.

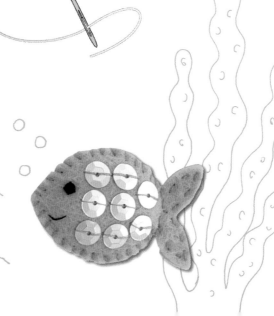

Wally the Jolly Whale

This is a very happy whale! Easy to sew and stuff, he's a great sea-dwelling animal to start with if you're a beginner. You could make Wally even easier to sew by skipping the blue stitched lines on the tail fin and the belly. Or you could add extra detail by adding some blue sequins to the body, sewing each sequin in place with three stitches of matching blue sewing thread.

You will need:

Templates on page 118

Blue felt, approx. 4 x 4¾in (10 x 12cm)

Light blue felt, approx. 1¼ x 2½in (3 x 6.5cm)

Small pieces of white and black felt

Matching sewing threads

Light blue and blue embroidery floss (thread)

Polyester stuffing

Needles, scissors, pins

1 Using the templates, cut out two whales and one fin from blue felt, one belly from light blue felt, and one eye from white felt. Cut out a small circle for the pupil from black felt (see page 9 for tips on cutting out small shapes).

2 Sew the eye and pupil onto one of the whale pieces using whipstitch (see page 10) in matching sewing threads. Pin the belly onto the whale as pictured, then whipstitch along the top edge using matching light blue sewing thread. Remove the pin.

3 Whipstitch the fin to the whale using matching blue sewing thread, then backstitch (see page 10) the whale's smile using a double thickness of black sewing thread, sewing flush with the right-hand edge of the belly.

4 Cut a length of light blue embroidery floss and separate half the strands (so for six-stranded floss, use three strands). Switch to a larger needle if necessary and backstitch two slightly curved lines onto the tail fin.

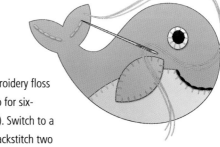

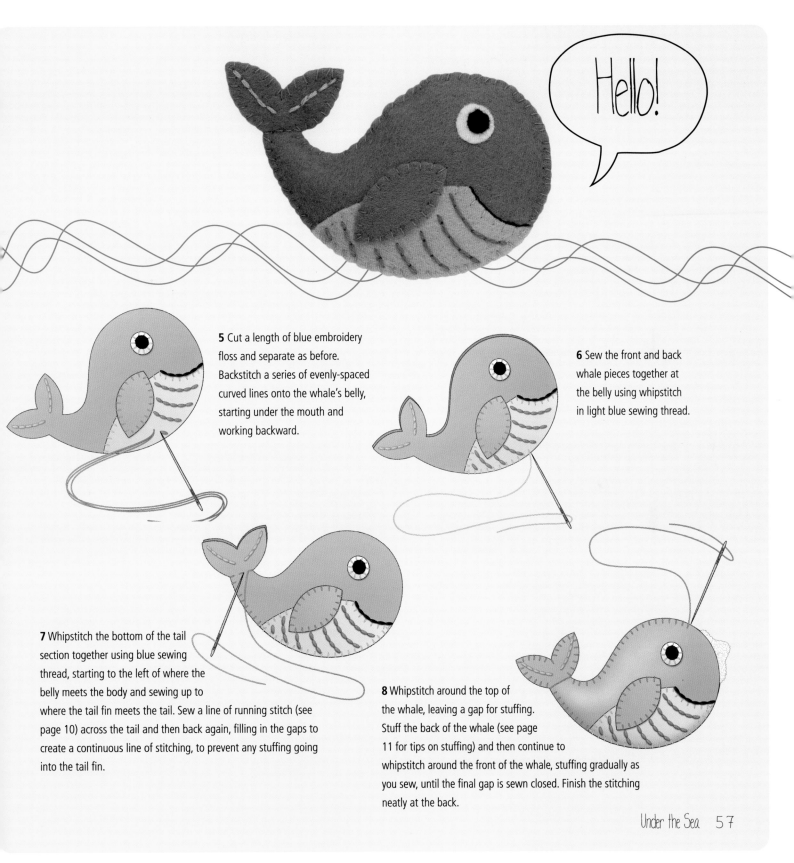

Hello!

5 Cut a length of blue embroidery floss and separate as before. Backstitch a series of evenly-spaced curved lines onto the whale's belly, starting under the mouth and working backward.

6 Sew the front and back whale pieces together at the belly using whipstitch in light blue sewing thread.

7 Whipstitch the bottom of the tail section together using blue sewing thread, starting to the left of where the belly meets the body and sewing up to where the tail fin meets the tail. Sew a line of running stitch (see page 10) across the tail and then back again, filling in the gaps to create a continuous line of stitching, to prevent any stuffing going into the tail fin.

8 Whipstitch around the top of the whale, leaving a gap for stuffing. Stuff the back of the whale (see page 11 for tips on stuffing) and then continue to whipstitch around the front of the whale, stuffing gradually as you sew, until the final gap is sewn closed. Finish the stitching neatly at the back.

Sam the Dainty Seahorse

A sweet little seahorse made using yellow and orange felt, but you could use any two bright colors you fancy. Why not use a third color for the line of stitches, or sew a row of colorful seed beads down the back of the seahorse instead?

You will need:

Templates on page 118

Yellow felt, approx. 3¾ x 3¾in (9.5 x 9.5cm)

Small pieces of white and black felt

Orange felt, approx. 1¾ x 3¾in (4.5 x 9.5cm)

Matching sewing threads

Orange embroidery floss (thread)

Polyester stuffing

Needles, scissors, pins

1 Using the templates, cut out two seahorses from yellow felt, one eye from white felt, and one fin and one row of spikes from orange felt. Cut out a small circle for the pupil from black felt (see page 9 for tips on cutting out small shapes).

2 Pin the spikes onto the back of one of the seahorse pieces so that the spikes are visible when you turn the seahorse over but the main band of orange felt is hidden. Sew the spikes in place using whipstitch (see page 10) in matching yellow sewing thread, sewing into the yellow felt but not through it. Remove the pins as you sew and set the seahorse aside.

3 Sew the eye and pupil onto the second seahorse piece using whipstitch in matching sewing threads, then backstitch (see page 10) the seahorse's smile using black sewing thread.

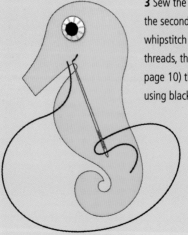

4 Sew the fin to the second seahorse piece by whipstitching along the inside edge using matching orange sewing thread.

5 Cut a length of orange embroidery floss and separate half the strands (so for six-stranded floss, use three strands). Switch to a larger needle if necessary and sew a row of single stitches down the back of the second seahorse and around the curved tail, taking care not to pull the stitches too tight to avoid puckering the felt.

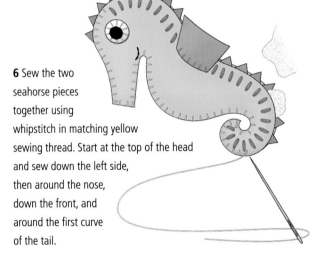

6 Sew the two seahorse pieces together using whipstitch in matching yellow sewing thread. Start at the top of the head and sew down the left side, then around the nose, down the front, and around the first curve of the tail.

7 Whipstitch the tail together, stuffing gradually as you sew around the curve (see page 11 for tips on stuffing). Stuff the nose and continue sewing up the back, stuffing as you sew until you have sewn up the final gap. Turn the seahorse back and forth as you sew past the orange spikes to ensure the stitching is neat on both sides, finishing neatly at the back.

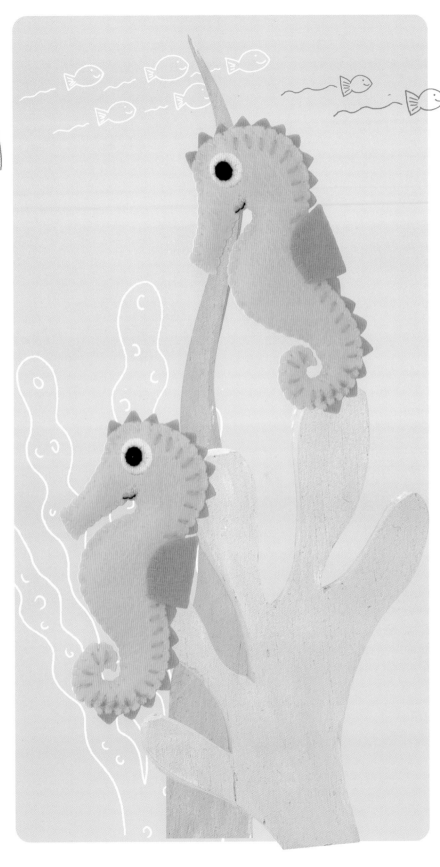

Dennis the Dancing Crab

This little crab is very happy to meet you, and unlike a real crab he won't snap at your fingers when saying hello! He would make a great gift for people born under the star sign of Cancer. For some added sparkle, sew red sequins on the crab's body between steps 2 and 3.

You will need:

Templates on page 119

Red felt, approx. 4¾ x 5¾in (12 x 14.5cm)

White, black, and red sewing thread

2 black seed beads, size 8/0

Polyester stuffing

Needle, scissors, pins

1 Using the templates, cut out two bodies, four legs, four arms, and two pincers from red felt. Cut out two eyes from white felt.

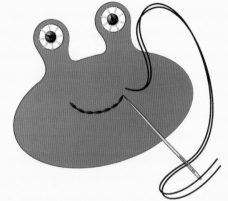

2 Sew an eye onto each eyestalk of one of the body shapes using whipstitch (see page 10) in white sewing thread. Sew a black seed bead pupil to each eye with three or four stitches of black sewing thread, then use a double thickness of black thread to backstitch (see page 10) the crab's smile.

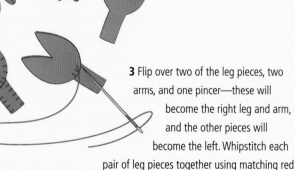

3 Flip over two of the leg pieces, two arms, and one pincer—these will become the right leg and arm, and the other pieces will become the left. Whipstitch each pair of leg pieces together using matching red sewing thread, leaving the top edges unstitched. Sew the two pincer shapes onto the corresponding arm shapes with a few whipstitches, then whipstitch the matching arm shapes together, starting and finishing the stitching at the bottom of each arm.

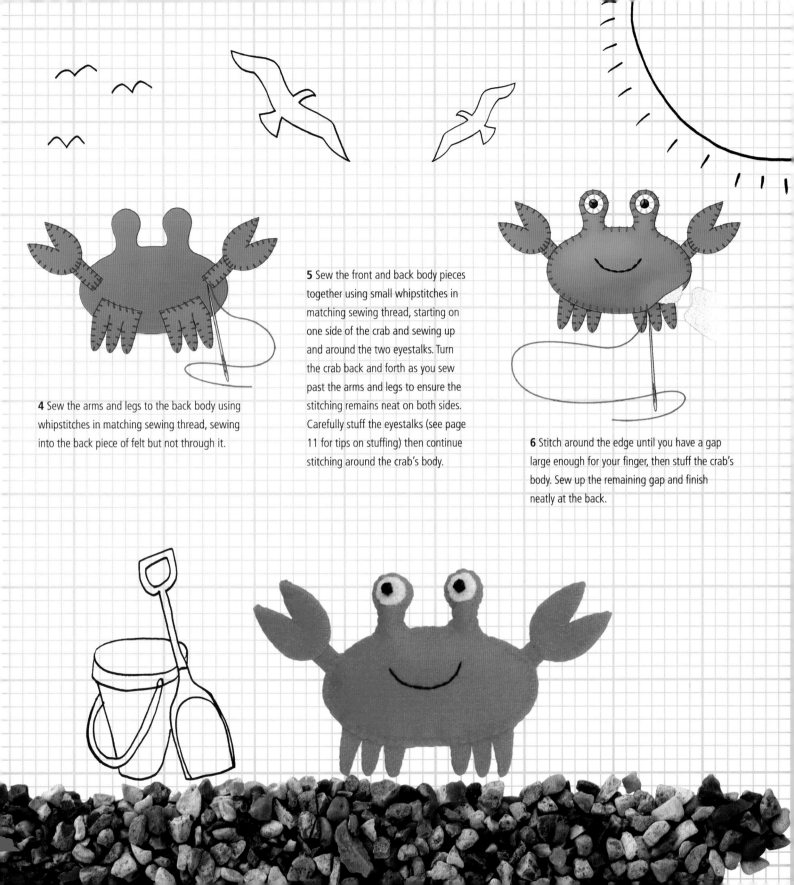

4 Sew the arms and legs to the back body using whipstitches in matching sewing thread, sewing into the back piece of felt but not through it.

5 Sew the front and back body pieces together using small whipstitches in matching sewing thread, starting on one side of the crab and sewing up and around the two eyestalks. Turn the crab back and forth as you sew past the arms and legs to ensure the stitching remains neat on both sides. Carefully stuff the eyestalks (see page 11 for tips on stuffing) then continue stitching around the crab's body.

6 Stitch around the edge until you have a gap large enough for your finger, then stuff the crab's body. Sew up the remaining gap and finish neatly at the back.

Delilah the Friendly Dolphin

Look who's leaping from the sea to wave hello! The dolphin is quite a simple project to sew but can be a little tricky to stuff as he's got lots of small fins at different angles, so take your time sewing him together. You could add some sparkle to your dolphin with some silver sequins, or sew him in two shades of blue instead of gray.

You will need:

Templates on page 119

Gray felt, approx. 4½ x 4¾in (11 x 12cm)

Pale gray felt, approx. 1¼ x 3¾in (3 x 9.5cm)

Small pieces of white and black felt

Gray, white, and black sewing threads

Polyester stuffing

Needle, scissors, pins

1 Using the templates, cut out one front body, one back body, and one fin from gray felt, one belly from pale gray felt, and one eye from white felt. Cut out a small circle for the pupil from black felt (see page 9 for tips on cutting out small shapes).

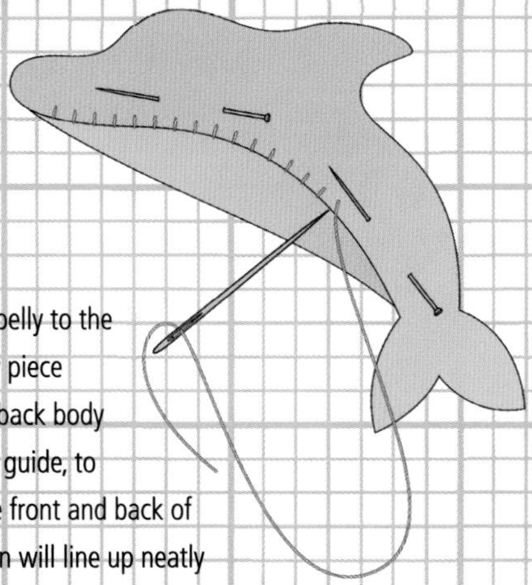

2 Pin the belly to the front body piece using the back body piece as a guide, to ensure the front and back of the dolphin will line up neatly when sewn together. Whipstitch (see page 10) the belly in place using matching gray sewing thread, then remove the pins.

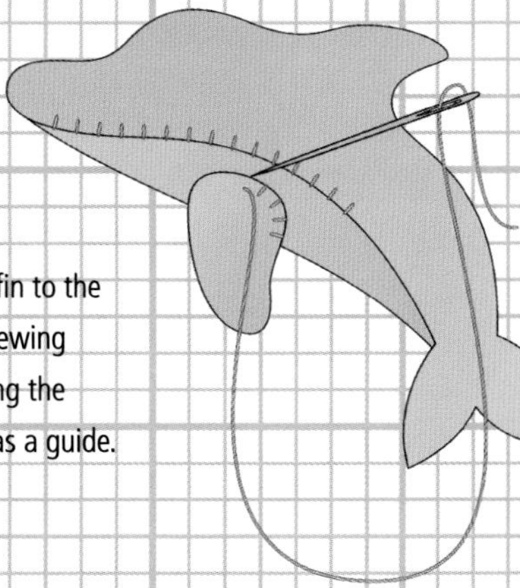

3 Whipstitch the fin to the belly using gray sewing thread, again using the back body piece as a guide.

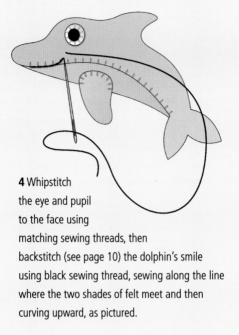

4 Whipstitch the eye and pupil to the face using matching sewing threads, then backstitch (see page 10) the dolphin's smile using black sewing thread, sewing along the line where the two shades of felt meet and then curving upward, as pictured.

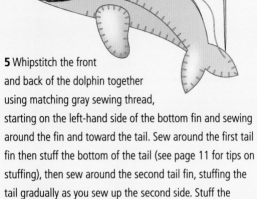

5 Whipstitch the front and back of the dolphin together using matching gray sewing thread, starting on the left-hand side of the bottom fin and sewing around the fin and toward the tail. Sew around the first tail fin then stuff the bottom of the tail (see page 11 for tips on stuffing), then sew around the second tail fin, stuffing the tail gradually as you sew up the second side. Stuff the dolphin's bottom fin.

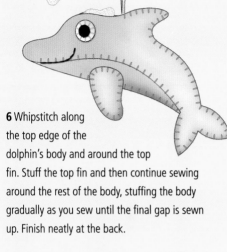

6 Whipstitch along the top edge of the dolphin's body and around the top fin. Stuff the top fin and then continue sewing around the rest of the body, stuffing the body gradually as you sew until the final gap is sewn up. Finish neatly at the back.

Wheeee!

Jasper the Sparkly Jellyfish

A sparkly jellyfish who just wants to smile at you, not sting you! This jellyfish has felt tentacles but you could use pretty pink ribbons and decorative trims instead. If you enlarge the jellyfish, draw all the shapes from step 4 on a piece of paper and enlarge them by the same percentage that you've used to enlarge the main templates.

You will need:

Templates on page 119

Pink felt, approx. 4½ x 5½in (11 x 14cm)

Small pieces of white and black felt

Matching sewing threads

Pink sequins, approx. ¼in (6mm) diameter

Polyester stuffing

Needle, scissors, pins

1 Using the templates, cut out two jellyfish from pink felt and two eyes from white felt. Cut six narrow strips approximately 3in (7.5cm) long and ¼in (5mm) wide for the tentacles and a rectangle measuring approximately 2in (5cm) wide and 3in (7.5cm) long from pink felt. Also cut two small circles for the pupils from black felt (see page 9 for tips on cutting out small shapes).

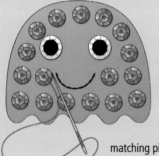

2 Sew the eyes and pupils in position on one of the jellyfish shapes using whipstitch (see page 10) in matching sewing threads, then use black sewing thread to backstitch (see page 10) the jellyfish's smile.

3 Sew pink sequins onto the jellyfish using three stitches of matching pink sewing thread to secure each one as pictured, being careful not to position the sequins too close to the edge of the felt.

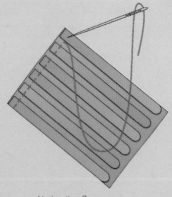

4 Shape one end of each of the tentacles into a curve so each tentacle is now approximately 2½in. (6.5cm) long. Arrange the tentacles onto the rectangle of pink felt as pictured, and sew them in place with a line of running stitch (see page 10) along the top edge.

5 Sew a line of running stitch down each tentacle and then back up again, filling in the gaps to create a continuous line of stitching. Turn the felt back and forth as you sew to ensure the stitching is neat on both sides.

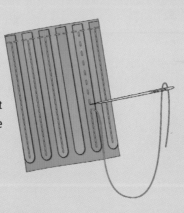

6 Cut around the tentacles carefully leaving a band of felt across the top approximately ½in (1.5cm) deep to create a set of six tentacles which are two layers thick.

Note: If you prefer to use ribbons for the jellyfish tentacles, skip steps 4, 5, and 6 and instead cut several pieces of narrow pink ribbon approximately 2½in (6.5cm) long and ¼in (5mm) wide, cutting the ends at an angle to help prevent fraying. Use running stitch to sew the ribbon ends to a strip of felt measuring approximately 2in (5cm) wide and ½in (1.5cm) deep.

7 Sew the tentacles to the back jellyfish piece with a line of whipstitch in matching sewing thread along the top edge, sewing into the back piece of felt but not through it.

8 Sew the front and the back jellyfish pieces together using whipstitch in matching sewing thread, starting toward the top on one side and sewing around the jellyfish and leaving a gap large enough for your finger. Turn the jellyfish back and forth as you sew past the tentacles to ensure the stitching is neat on both sides. Stuff the jellyfish (see page 11 for tips on stuffing), sew up the remaining gap and finish neatly at the back.

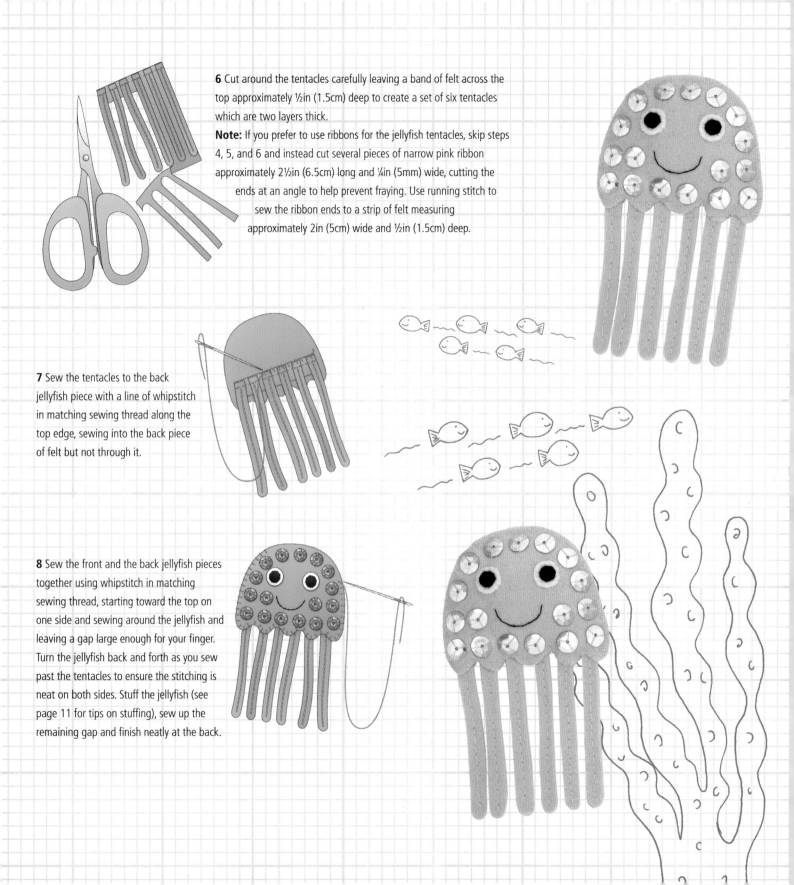

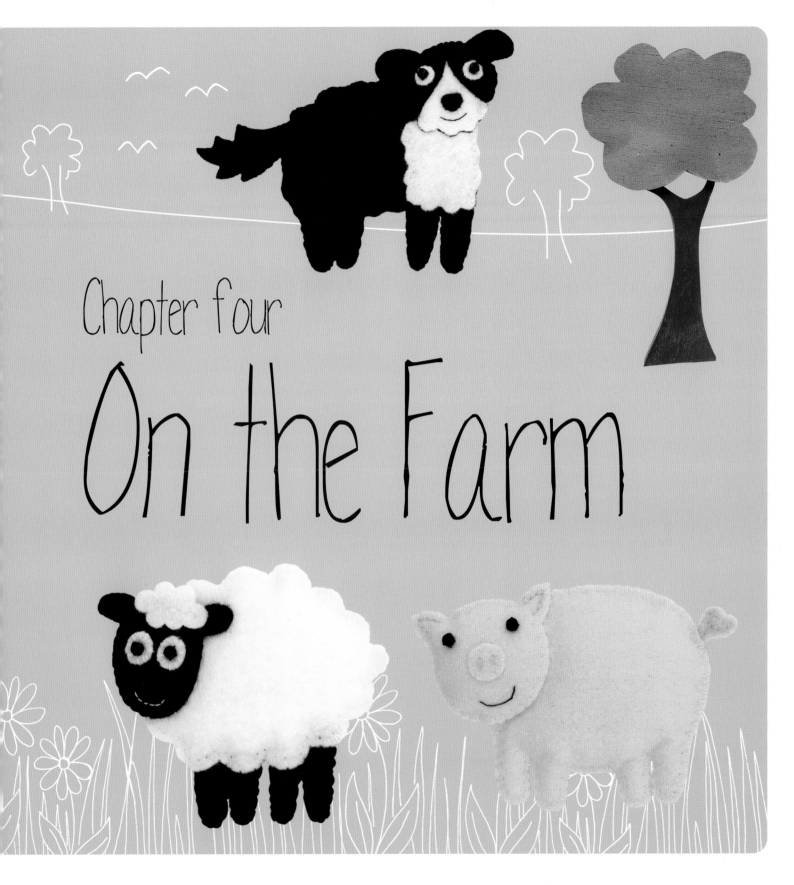

Chapter four

On the Farm

The Chicken Family

A mother hen and her two little chicks. The hen is made using black and white felt, but you could make a brown chicken by using two shades of brown felt and a contrasting shade of brown embroidery floss to add the feather details. You could also add some extra stitching on the wing. I used bright yellow thread to sew both my chicks, but you can use matching pale yellow thread for the pale yellow chick, if you prefer.

You will need:

Templates on page 120

White felt, approx. 4 x 5¼in (10 x 13.5cm)

Orange felt, approx. 2½ x 3in (6.5 x 8cm)

Red felt, approx. 1¾ x 1¼in (4.5 x 4.5cm)

Small piece of black felt

Yellow felt, approx. 3 x 3¼in (8 x 8.5cm)

Pale yellow felt, approx. 3 x 3¼in (8 x 8.5cm)

Matching sewing threads

Black embroidery floss (thread)

2 black seed beads, size 9/0

Polyester stuffing

Needles, scissors, pins

The Chicken

1 Using the templates, cut out two chickens, one wing, and one eye from white felt, one beak and a set of legs from orange felt, and one comb and one face from red felt. Cut out a small circle for the pupil from black felt (see page 9 for tips on cutting out small shapes).

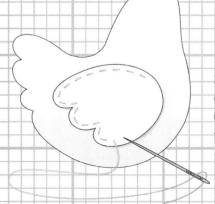

2 Sew the wing onto one of the chicken pieces using running stitch (see page 10) and white sewing thread.

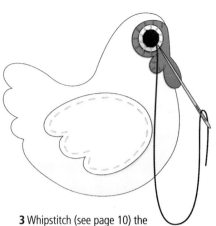

3 Whipstitch (see page 10) the face piece onto the chicken, as pictured, using matching red sewing thread and leaving the bottom section of the face (the wattle) unstitched. Whipstitch the eye and pupil to the face using matching sewing threads.

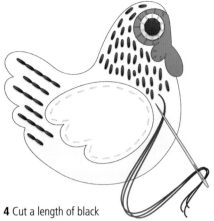

4 Cut a length of black embroidery floss and separate half the strands (so for six-stranded floss, use three strands). Switch to a larger needle if necessary and backstitch (see page 10) a set of lines onto the tail for the tail feathers, then sew a series of small single stitches onto the chicken's head and chest.

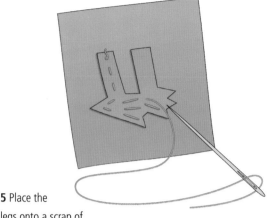

5 Place the legs onto a scrap of matching orange felt. Starting at the top of one of the legs sew the legs to the backing felt using running stitch (see page 10) in matching orange sewing thread. Follow the outline of the legs and turn the felt back and forth as you sew to ensure the stitching is neat on both sides. Cut around the leg shape to create a pair of legs that are two layers thick.

6 Whipstitch the legs, comb, and beak onto the back chicken piece using white sewing thread, sewing into the white felt but not through it.

7 Place the front and back of the chicken together and whipstitch the edge of the red face section using matching red sewing thread, leaving the wattle unstitched. Turn the chicken back and forth as you sew past the beak to ensure the stitching is neat on both sides.

8 Starting from just above the face, whipstitch around the chicken using white sewing thread, stuffing the chicken gradually as you sew up the belly (see page 11 for tips on stuffing). Turn the chicken back and forth as you sew past the comb and legs to ensure the stitching is neat on both sides, and when you reach the red face again lift up the red wattle as you sew behind it. Finish neatly at the back.

The Chicks

1 Using the templates, for each chick cut out two chicks and one wing from yellow or pale yellow felt, and one beak and one set of feet from orange felt.

Note: The chicks have a single layer of felt for their feet, but to make them thicker or sturdier cut out an extra foot piece and sew the two layers together with running stitch (see page 10) or whipstitch (see page 10) in matching orange sewing thread. Or, if you find sewing two small pieces together a bit tricky, use the method for sewing the larger chicken's legs (opposite).

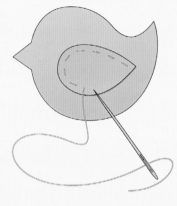

2 Sew the wing onto one of the chick pieces using running stitch (see page 10) and yellow sewing thread.

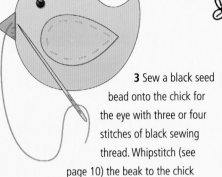

3 Sew a black seed bead onto the chick for the eye with three or four stitches of black sewing thread. Whipstitch (see page 10) the beak to the chick using matching orange sewing thread.

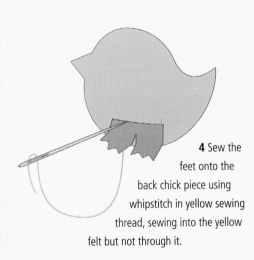

4 Sew the feet onto the back chick piece using whipstitch in yellow sewing thread, sewing into the yellow felt but not through it.

5 Whipstitch the front and back of the chick together at the beak using matching orange sewing thread.

6 Starting from just below the beak, whipstitch around the chick using yellow sewing thread, leaving a small gap for stuffing. Stuff the chick (see page 11 for tips on stuffing) and sew up the final gap, finishing neatly at the back.

Alfred the Awesome Pig

Oink! Oink! This fat little pig is simple to sew and easy to stuff, making him a good farm animal to start with if you're a beginner. If you want you can skip steps 5, 6, and 7 and instead embroider a curly tail directly onto the back of the pig.

You will need:

Templates on page 120

Pale pink felt, approx. 4¾ x 5¼in (12 x 13.5cm)

Black and pale pink sewing thread

Light pink embroidery floss (thread)

Two black seed beads, size 8/0

Polyester stuffing

Needles, scissors, pins

1 Using the templates, cut out one front body piece, one back body piece, one head, and one nose from pale pink felt.

2 Position the head on the front body piece, using the back body piece as a guide so that the front and back of the pig will match up when you sew them together later. Whipstitch (see page 10) the head in place using matching pale pink sewing thread.

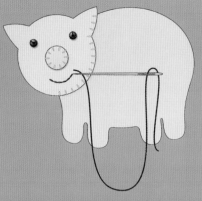

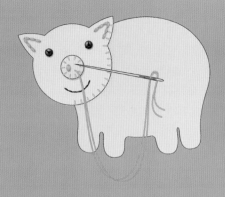

3 Sew the nose onto the face using whipstitch in pale pink sewing thread, then sew on two black seed beads for the eyes with three or four stitches of black sewing thread. Backstitch (see page 10) a smile onto the face using black sewing thread.

4 Cut a length of embroidery floss and separate two strands. Backstitch a slightly curved upside-down V shape onto both of the pig's ears, then sew three small stitches on top of each other on the nose to form each of the pig's nostrils.

5 Cut another length of embroidery floss and separate half the strands (so for six-stranded floss, use three strands). Backstitch a small loop onto a scrap of pale pink felt as pictured, to form a curly tail about ½in (1.5cm) long.

6 Cut out the stitched tail, leaving a bit of extra felt on the left hand side. Place the tail onto another scrap of pale pink felt and sew the layers together using running stitch in matching sewing thread. Turn the felt back and forth as you sew to ensure the stitching is neat on both sides. Cut around the tail shape to create a tail that's two layers thick.

7 Sew the tail to the back body piece using whipstitches in matching sewing thread, sewing into the back piece of felt but not through it.

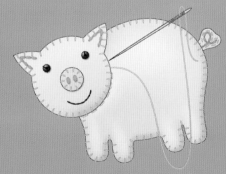

9 If you wish, sew a line of running stitch (see page 10) flush around the edge of the pig's head from the bottom of the head up toward the top using matching sewing thread, to improve the shape. Carefully sew through all the layers of felt and stuffing to pull the layers closer together. Turn the pig back and forth as you sew to ensure the stitching is neat on both sides. Finish neatly at the back.

8 Sew the front and back body pieces together using whipstitch in matching sewing thread, starting from the left-hand side where the head meets the body and sewing along the bottom of the pig and around the legs. Stuff the legs (see page 11 for tips on stuffing) then continue to sew around the pig, stuffing gradually until you've closed up the final gap.

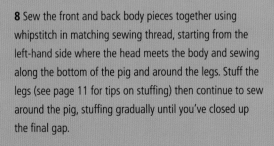

Sheelagh the Shy Sheep

Baa! Meet a very fluffy sheep! You could vary the colors by using cream felt for the face and legs instead of black, or dark gray felt for the fleece and fluff on the sheep's head. Add some sparkle to the sheep by sewing white or silver sequins onto the white fleece.

You will need:

Templates on page 121

Black felt, approx. 3¼ x 3¾in (8.5 x 9.5cm)

White felt, approx. 3 x 4¾in (8 x 12cm)

Matching sewing thread

2 black seed beads, size 8/0

Polyester stuffing

Needle, scissors, pins

1 Using the templates, cut out two leg pieces, one front head, and one back head from black felt, and two fleeces, two eyes, and one fluff piece from white felt.

2 Sew the front head onto one of the fleeces using whipstitch (see page 10) in black sewing thread, sewing up the right-hand edge of the head and past the ear instead of around it.

3 Pin the back head shape onto the second fleece so it overlaps the head as pictured, using the sewn-together front pieces as a guide to ensure the front and back of the sheep will match up when sewn together. Sew in place using whipstitch in white sewing thread, and remove the pin.

4 Whipstitch the eyes to the front head piece using white sewing thread then sew the fluff to the head with a horizontal line of running stitch (see page 10), being careful not to sew too close to the edge of the head. Sew two black seed beads to the eyes for the pupils with three or four stitches of black sewing thread, then backstitch (see page 10) the sheep's smile using white sewing thread.

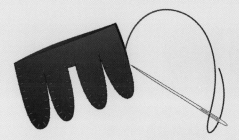

5 Whipstitch the two leg pieces together using black sewing thread, leaving the top edge open, then stuff each leg up to where it joins the horizontal band of felt that runs across the top of the shape (see page 10 for tips on stuffing).

6 Sew the legs to the back of the back body piece with a line of whipstitch along the top edge of the legs in white sewing thread, sewing into the white felt but not through it.

7 Sew the front and back of the sheep together at the head using whipstitch in black sewing thread, sewing past the ear as before and folding the white fluff forward as you sew behind it.

8 Whipstitch around the bottom of the fleece in white sewing thread, starting under the head and turning the sheep back and forth as you sew past the legs to ensure the stitching is neat on both sides. Stuff the bottom of the sheep and sew around to the head, stuffing gradually as you sew until the final gap is closed.

9 If you wish, sew a line of running stitch in white sewing thread flush around the edge of the sheep's head, from top to bottom, to improve the shape. Carefully sew through all the layers of felt and stuffing to pull the layers closer together. Turn the sheep back and forth as you sew to ensure the stitching is neat on both sides, and fold the sheep's ear forward as you sew behind it. Finish the stitching neatly at the back.

Clive the Clever Sheepdog

This smart Border Collie works hard to keep the sheep in order! If you're making more than one sheepdog you can vary their coloring by adding different white patches to their coats.

You will need:

Templates on page 122

White felt, approx. 2 x 2½in (5 x 6.5cm)

Black felt, approx. 3¾ x 6¾in (9.5 x 16.5cm)

Matching sewing threads

2 black seed beads, size 8/0

Polyester stuffing

Needle, scissors, pins

1 Using the templates, cut out one head and one chest from white felt and one front body, one back body, one of each face patch, two ears, and two tails from black felt. Cut out two small circles for the eyes from white felt, and a small rounded triangle for the nose from black felt (see page 9 for tips on cutting out small shapes).

2 Pin or hold the chest and head onto the front body piece, as pictured, using the back body piece as a guide so that the front and back of the sheepdog will line up neatly when sewn together. Whipstitch (see page 10) the chest and head to the front body using white sewing thread then remove the pin, if you've used one.

3 Whipstitch the two patches to the head using black sewing thread.

4 Whipstitch the ears in place using black sewing thread, so most of the ear flaps free from the head, then backstitch a line flush with the edge of the sheepdog's head to clearly divide the white face and white chest.

5 Whipstitch the eyes and nose to the face using matching sewing threads. Sew two black seed beads to the eyes with three or four stitches of black sewing thread, then backstitch (see page 10) the sheepdog's smile.

6 Place the two tail pieces together and whipstitch around the edge using black sewing thread.

7 Whipstitch the tail to the back body piece using black sewing thread, sewing into the back piece of felt but not through it.

8 Sew the front and back of the sheepdog together using whipstitch in black sewing thread, starting on the left where the tail meets the body and sewing around the legs until you reach the white felt of the chest. Stuff the legs (see page 11 for tips on stuffing).

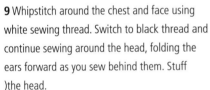

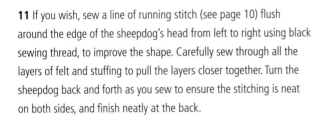

9 Whipstitch around the chest and face using white sewing thread. Switch to black thread and continue sewing around the head, folding the ears forward as you sew behind them. Stuff)the head.

10 Whipstitch across the sheepdog's back from the tail to the head, stuffing gradually as you sew until the final gap has been sewn up.

11 If you wish, sew a line of running stitch (see page 10) flush around the edge of the sheepdog's head from left to right using black sewing thread, to improve the shape. Carefully sew through all the layers of felt and stuffing to pull the layers closer together. Turn the sheepdog back and forth as you sew to ensure the stitching is neat on both sides, and finish neatly at the back.

Maisy the Marvelous Cow

A friendly cow who wants to say Mooo! (Hello!). This cow is made using black and white felt, but if you like you can make a brown cow by using brown instead of white felt and leaving off the patches. You could also make a more abstract dotty cow, cutting colorful circles of felt for the patches, or even using polka-dot felt.

You will need:

Templates on page 120

White felt, approx. 5¼ x 6½in (13.5 x 16cm)

Black felt, approx. 2½ x 3¼in (6.5 x 8.5cm)

Pale pink felt, approx. 2 x 2½in (5 x 6.5cm)

Matching sewing threads

Black sequins, ¼in (6mm) diameter

Polyester stuffing

Needle, scissors, pins

1 Using the templates, cut out one front body, one back body, one head, two eyes, and one tail from white felt, one of each of the three patches (A, B, and C) and the left and right face patches from black felt, and two udders and one muzzle from pale pink felt. Cut out two circles for the pupils from black felt (see page 9 for tips on cutting out small shapes).

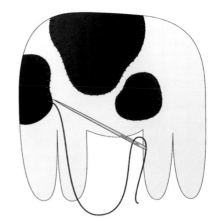

2 Whipstitch (see page 10) the three black patches (A, B, and C) onto the front body piece using black sewing thread.

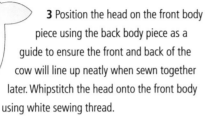

3 Position the head on the front body piece using the back body piece as a guide to ensure the front and back of the cow will line up neatly when sewn together later. Whipstitch the head onto the front body using white sewing thread.

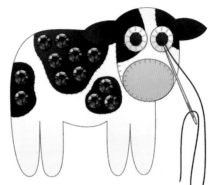

4 Sew black sequins onto the black patches using three stitches of black sewing thread to secure each one, taking care not to position the sequins too close to the edge of the cow's body.

5 Whipstitch the two black face patches, the pink muzzle, and the eyes and pupils onto the cow's head using matching sewing threads.

6 Backstitch (see page 10 two circles onto the muzzle to form the cow's nostrils using matching pale pink sewing thread, then backstitch the cow's smile using black sewing thread.

7 Backstitch around the cow's eyes using black sewing thread. If you wish, sew a line of backstitch flush around the edge of the cow's head and ear using white sewing thread —this will help the head clearly stand out from the black patch on the cow's body.

8 Place the tail onto a scrap piece of white felt. Starting at the top of the tail, sew a line of running stitch (see page 10) in white thread to the bottom and back again, filling in the gaps between the stitches to create a continuous line, as pictured. Turn the felt back and forth as you sew to ensure the stitching is neat on both sides. Cut around the tail shape to create a tail that's two layers thick.

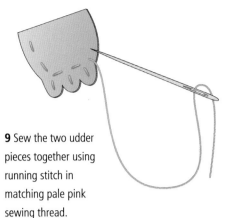

9 Sew the two udder pieces together using running stitch in matching pale pink sewing thread.

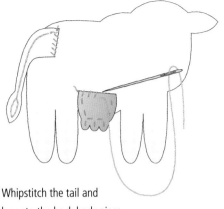

10 Whipstitch the tail and udder onto the back body piece using white sewing thread, sewing into the white felt but not through it.

11 Sew the front and back of the cow together using whipstitch in white sewing thread, starting on the left-hand side (just underneath the black patch) and sewing around the legs and up to just under the cow's head. Stuff the legs (see page 11 for tips on stuffing).

12 Whipstitch up the back and around the head, stuffing the cow gradually as you sew and switching between black and white sewing thread as needed until you've sewn up the final gap. Turn the cow back and forth as you sew past the tail to ensure the stitching is neat on both sides.

13 If you wish, sew a line of running stitch flush around the edge of the cow's head from bottom to top using white sewing thread, to improve the shape. Carefully sew through all the layers of felt and stuffing to pull the layers closer together. Turn the cow back and forth as you sew to ensure the stitching is neat on both sides, finishing neatly at the back.

Horace the Happy Horse

Do you have a sugar cube for this lovely horse? This horse is made using brown felt, but you could make yours in any color you like by changing the shades you choose for the horse and its mane, for example pale gray with a darker gray mane. If you want to give your horse different markings, trace around the head and front body templates and sketch the markings you'd like to add. Cut these shapes out and use them as templates, then sew your pieces onto the horse with matching whipstitches in step 4.

You will need:

Templates on page 123

Dark brown felt, approx. 3 x 3¼in (8 x 8.5cm)

Small pieces of white and black felt

Brown felt, approx. 4½ x 6in (11 x 15cm)

Matching sewing threads

Polyester stuffing

Needle, scissors, pins

1 Using the templates, cut out one each of the mane (and the forelock) and two tails from dark brown felt, one blaze and two eyes from white felt, and one front body, one back body, one head, and one muzzle from brown felt. Cut out two small circles for the pupils from black felt (see page 9 for tips on cutting out small shapes).

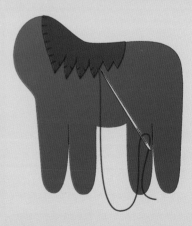

2 Whipstitch (see page 10) the mane onto the front body piece using matching dark brown sewing thread.

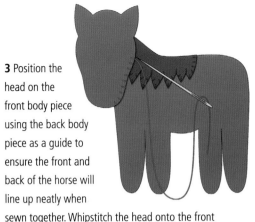

3 Position the head on the front body piece using the back body piece as a guide to ensure the front and back of the horse will line up neatly when sewn together. Whipstitch the head onto the front body using matching brown sewing thread.

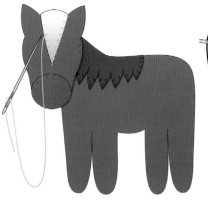

4 Whipstitch the muzzle and blaze onto the horse's head using matching sewing threads.

5 Whipstitch the forelock, eyes, and pupils in place using matching threads.

6 Backstitch (see page 10) two small circles onto the muzzle using dark brown sewing thread to form the nostrils, then backstitch the horse's smile using white sewing thread.

7 Place the two tail pieces together and whipstitch around the edges using matching dark brown sewing thread.

8 Whipstitch the tail to the back body piece using matching brown sewing thread, sewing into the brown felt but not through it.

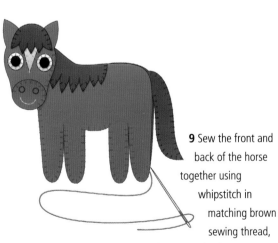

9 Sew the front and back of the horse together using whipstitch in matching brown sewing thread, starting at the left where the head meets its body. Sew around the legs and then stuff them (see page 11 for tips on stuffing).

10 Whipstitch along the horse's back and around the head, stuffing gradually as you sew until the final gap has been sewn up.

11 If you wish, sew a line of running stitch (see page 10) up the side of the horse's head, from bottom to top, using brown sewing thread to improve the shape. Carefully sew through all the layers of felt and stuffing to pull the layers closer together. Turn the horse back and forth as you sew to ensure the stitching is neat on both sides, and finish neatly at the back.

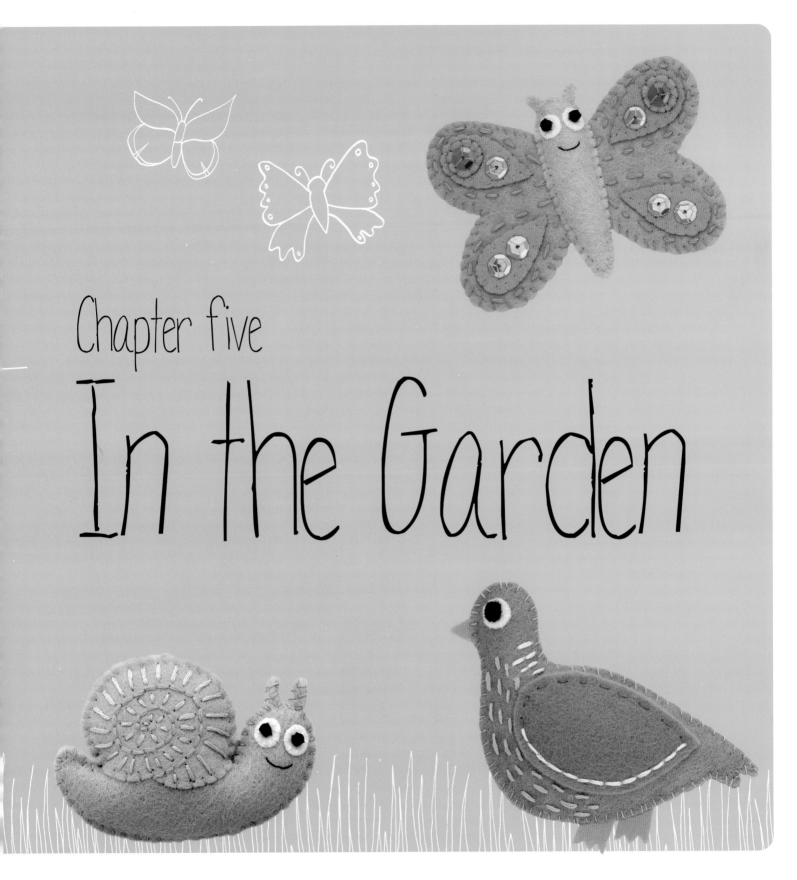

Chapter five

In the Garden

The Robin Family

A whole family of robins, including one chick that hasn't yet hatched completely. Even though these robins are based on British robins (who have white eggs), I thought the "robin's egg blue" of the American robin's eggs was too pretty not to be used! Add a ribbon loop to the mama robin (see page 12) to make a cute Christmas ornament.

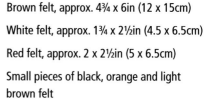

You will need:

Templates on page 124

Brown felt, approx. 4¾ x 6in (12 x 15cm)

White felt, approx. 1¾ x 2½in (4.5 x 6.5cm)

Red felt, approx. 2 x 2½in (5 x 6.5cm)

Small pieces of black, orange and light brown felt

Light turquoise felt, approx. 3 x 3¼in (8 x 8.5cm)

Matching sewing threads

Light brown embroidery floss (thread)

Red sequins, approx. ⅛in (8mm) diameter

4 black seed beads, size 8/0

Polyester stuffing

Needles, scissors, pins

The Robin

1 Using the templates, cut out two robins and wings from brown felt, one belly and two eyes from white felt, one chest from red felt, and one beak and four feet from black felt. Cut out two small circles for the pupils from black felt (see page 9 for tips on cutting out small shapes).

2 Pin the belly to the bottom of one of the robin pieces and whipstitch (see page 10) in place using white sewing thread. Remove the pin.

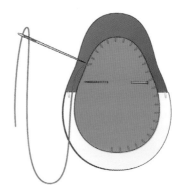

3 Pin the chest to the center of the robin and whipstitch in place using matching red sewing thread. Remove the pin.

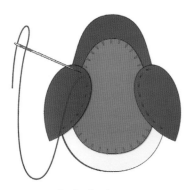

4 Attach the wings with a line of running stitch (see page 10) in matching brown sewing thread along the inside edges, taking care not to sew too close to the edge of the robin's body.

5 Sew the sequins to the robin's chest using three stitches of red sewing thread to secure each one. Sew the eyes, pupils, and beak to the face using whipstitch and matching sewing threads.

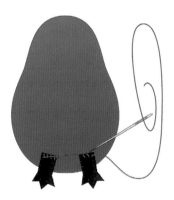

6 Turn over one pair of feet so you have two left and two right feet. Sew each matching pair together using whipstitch in black sewing thread, starting at the top of each foot and working around the edge until you reach the top again. Sew the feet to the back robin piece using whipstitch in matching brown sewing thread, sewing into the brown felt but not through it.

7 Sew the front and back robin pieces together using whipstitch in matching brown sewing thread, starting at one side near the top and sewing most of the way around but leaving a gap for stuffing. Bend the wings forward as you sew behind them and turn the robin back and forth as you sew past the feet to ensure the stitching is neat on both sides.

8 Stuff the robin (see page 11 for tips on stuffing) and sew up the gap, finishing neatly at the back.

The Egg

1 Using the templates, cut out two eggs from light turquoise felt.

2 Sew the two egg pieces together using whipstitch (see page 10) in matching light turquoise sewing thread. Sew most of the way around the edge then stuff the egg (see page 11 for tips on stuffing). Sew up the remaining gap, finishing neatly at the back.

The Baby Robin in an Egg

1 Using the templates, cut out two unhatched baby robins from brown felt and two eggshells from light turquoise felt. Cut out a small triangle for the beak from orange felt (see page 9 for tips on cutting out small shapes).

2 Turn over robin and one eggshell—these will form the back of the unhatched baby robin. Whipstitch (see page 10) the eggshells to their corresponding robins using matching light turquoise sewing thread, ensuring the front and back halves will match up perfectly when sewn together later.

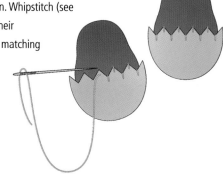

3 Sew two black seed beads onto the front of the robin for the eyes using three or four stitches of black sewing thread. Sew the beak in place using three stitches in matching orange sewing thread, sewing one stitch over each point of the triangle.

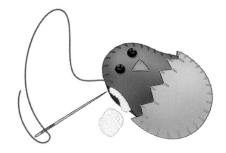

4 Sew the front and back of the eggshell together use whipstitches in matching light turquoise sewing thread. Sew the front and back of the robin together using whipstitches in matching brown sewing thread, leaving a small gap for stuffing. Stuff the robin and eggshell (see page 11 for tips on stuffing) and sew up the remaining gap, finishing neatly at the back.

The Baby Robin

1 Using the templates, cut out two baby robins from brown felt, two baby robin wings from light brown felt, and two baby robin feet from orange felt. Cut out a small triangle for the beak from orange felt (see page 9 for tips on cutting out small shapes).

Note: The baby robin has a single layer of felt for each foot, but to make the feet thicker or sturdier cut out four feet instead of two and sew the two layers together with running stitch (see page 10) or whipstitch (see page 10) in matching orange sewing thread. Or, if you find sewing two small pieces together a bit tricky, use the method for sewing the Owl's feet on page 20, sewing one shape onto a piece of felt and then cutting out the second layer after you've finished stitching.

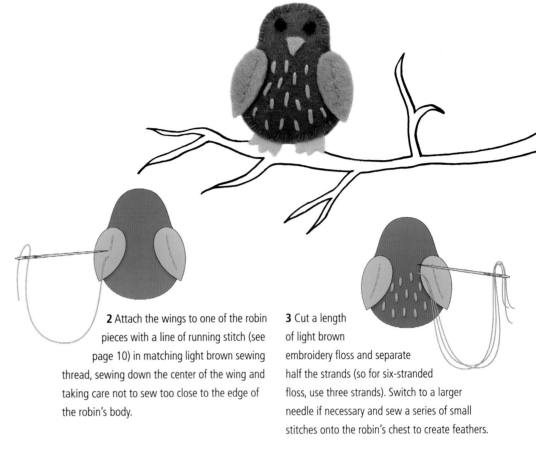

2 Attach the wings to one of the robin pieces with a line of running stitch (see page 10) in matching light brown sewing thread, sewing down the center of the wing and taking care not to sew too close to the edge of the robin's body.

3 Cut a length of light brown embroidery floss and separate half the strands (so for six-stranded floss, use three strands). Switch to a larger needle if necessary and sew a series of small stitches onto the robin's chest to create feathers.

4 Sew two black seed beads on the face for the eyes using three or four stitches of black sewing thread, then sew the beak in place with three stitches of matching orange sewing thread, sewing one stitch over each point of the triangle.

5 Sew the feet to the back body piece with a line of whipstitch (see page 10) in matching brown sewing thread, sewing into the back piece of felt but not through it.

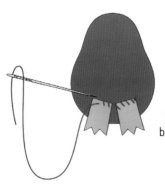

6 Sew the front and back body pieces together using whipstitch in brown sewing thread, starting near the top at one side and sewing around the robin leaving a gap for stuffing. Fold the wings forward as you sew behind them and turn the robin back and forth as you sew past the feet to ensure the stitching is neat on both sides. Stuff the robin (see page 11 for tips on stuffing), sew up the gap, and finish neatly at the back.

Frida the Forgetful Frog

Ribbit! Ribbit! This happy little frog is easy to sew, making it a great garden animal to start with if you're a beginner. If you'd prefer to sew a tropical frog, use bright lime green felt and decorate the frog with red sequins instead of green ones.

You will need:

Templates on page 122

Green felt, approx. 4½ x 4¾in (11 x 12cm)

Small pieces of white and black felt

Matching sewing threads

Green sequins, approx. ¼in (6mm) diameter

Polyester stuffing

Needle, scissors, pins

1 Using the templates, cut out two frogs and one of each leg shape from green felt, and one eye from white felt. Cut out a small black felt circle for the pupil (see page 9 for tips on cutting out small shapes).

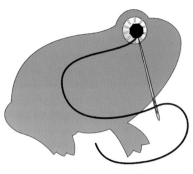

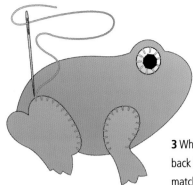

3 Whipstitch the front and back legs in place using matching sewing thread.

2 Sew the eye and pupil onto one of the frog shapes as pictured using whipstitch (see page 10) and matching sewing threads.

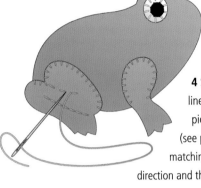

4 Sew two slightly curved lines onto the back leg as pictured in running stitch (see page 10) using matching thread. Sew in one direction and then sew back again filling in the gaps to create a continuous line of stitching.

5 Backstitch (see page 10) the frog's smile with small stitches in black sewing thread starting from the small indent in the frog shape, as pictured.

6 Starting at the top of the frog and working downward, sew the sequins in place with three stitches of matching sewing thread. Avoid sewing the sequins too close to the edge of the felt.

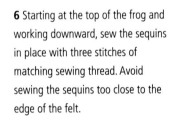

Ribbit!

7 Place the front and back of the frog together and sew along the bottom edge of the frog using whipstitch in matching thread. Stuff the bottom half of the body (see page 11 for tips on stuffing).

8 Continue sewing the frog together, stuffing gradually as you sew, and finishing neatly at the back.

Charles the Cheeky Pigeon

Coo! Coo! Pigeons are a bird that you either love or hate—I love them! This wood pigeon has lots of embroidered details, but you could also add some silver sequins to its wing if you like. Give him as a gift to a friend who, like me, is a fan of pigeons... or send him in a letter to turn it into "pigeon post."

You will need:

Templates on page 123

Light gray felt, approx. 3¼ x 4in (8.5 x 10cm)

Gray felt, approx. 1¼ x 2in (3 x 5cm)

Small pieces of white, orange, and black felt

Matching sewing threads

White and lilac embroidery floss (thread)

Polyester stuffing

Needles, scissors, pins

1 Using the templates, cut out two pigeons from light gray felt, one wing from gray felt, one eye from white felt, and one beak and two feet from orange felt. Cut out a small oval for the pupil from black felt (see page 9 for tips on cutting out small shapes).

Note: This pigeon has a single layer of felt for the beak and each foot, but to make them thicker or sturdier cut out an extra beak and pair of feet and sew the two layers together with running stitch (see page 10) or whipstitch (see page 10) in matching orange sewing thread. Or, if you find sewing two small pieces together a bit tricky, use the method for sewing the Owl's feet on page 20, sewing one shape onto a piece of felt and then cutting out the second layer after you've finished stitching.

2 Sew the eye and pupil onto one of the pigeon pieces using whipstitch (see page 10) in matching white and black sewing threads.

3 Pin or hold the wing in place and sew a line of running stitch (see page 10) around the outside in matching gray sewing thread. Remove the pin, if you've used one.

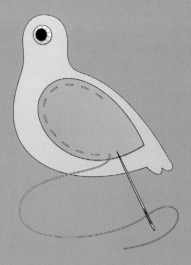

4 Cut a length of lilac embroidery floss and separate half the strands (so for six-stranded floss, use three strands). Switch to a larger needle if necessary and sew three lines of single stitches up the belly and neck of the pigeon, varying the length of the stitches slightly. Cut a length of white embroidery floss and separate the strands as before. Sew four very short rows of stitches on the pigeon's neck, and backstitch (see page 10) a line along the bottom edge of the wing, as pictured.

5 Sew the beak and feet onto the back pigeon piece using whipstitch in matching light gray sewing thread, sewing into the back piece of felt but not through it.

6 Sew the front and back pigeon pieces together using whipstitch in matching light gray sewing thread, starting to the left of the feet and sewing past the tail and then up and around the head. Turn the pigeon back and forth as you sew past the feet and beak to ensure the stitching is neat on both sides.

7 Stuff the head, neck, and tail (see page 11 for tips on stuffing) then stitch around the belly, stuffing gradually until the final gap has been closed up and finishing neatly at the back.

Coo! Coo!

Boris the Beautiful Butterfly

A cute butterfly with very colorful wings! You can make a whole set of unique butterflies by varying the color of the wings as well as the sequins and embroidery stitches. Use the templates to draw the outline of the butterfly onto a piece of paper, then make copies and use them to plan out lots of different wing designs.

You will need:

Templates on page 124

Turquoise felt, approx. 4 x 5¼in (10 x 13.5cm)

Coral felt, approx. 1¾ x 3in (4.5 x 8cm)

Light turquoise felt, approx. 2 x 2½in (5 x 6.5cm)

Small piece of white felt

Matching sewing threads and black thread

Bright pink embroidery floss (thread)

2 bright pink and 6 blue sequins, approx. ¼in (6mm) diameter

2 black seed beads, size 8/0

Polyester stuffing

Needles, scissors, pins

1 Using the templates, cut out two wings and two circles from turquoise felt, two top teardrops and two bottom teardrops from coral felt, and two bodies from light turquoise felt, and two eyes from white felt.

2 Pin one of the body shapes in the center of the wings, as pictured. Whipstitch (see page 10) the teardrop shapes to the wings using matching coral sewing thread, and the circles on top of the upper teardrops using matching turquoise thread.

3 Sew a pink sequin onto each circle and blue sequins onto the teardrops, as pictured, using three stitches in matching thread to secure each one. For symmetry, ensure the stitches on the right wing mirror those on the left.

4 Cut a length of bright pink embroidery floss and separate half the strands (so for six-stranded floss, use three strands). Switch to a larger needle if necessary and sew a line of small running stitches (see page 10) around each teardrop, starting and ending the stitching flush with the edge of the butterfly's body.

5 Remove the pin and set the wings aside. Using white sewing thread, whipstitch the eyes into position on one body piece. Sew a black seed bead pupil to each eye with three or four stitches of black sewing thread. Backstitch a smile onto the face using black sewing thread.

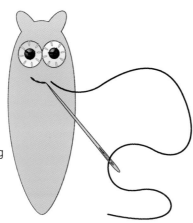

6 Place all four layers on top of each other, so the wings are sandwiched between the two body pieces, and pin them together. Starting from where the bottom of one of the wings meets the body, whipstitch one side of the body together using matching sewing thread. Sew up to the head and around the antennae, turning the butterfly back and forth as you sew to ensure the stitches are neat on both sides. Remove the pin.

7 Whipstitch down the other side of the butterfly's body, stuffing the body gradually as you sew (see page 11 for tips on stuffing), until the whole body is stuffed and you've stitched all the way around the edge.

8 Whipstitch the edges of the wings together using matching sewing thread. The butterfly pictured has flat wings, but if you'd like to stuff the wings, leave a gap large enough for your finger in each wing and stuff the wings lightly before sewing the gaps closed. Finish the stitching neatly at the back.

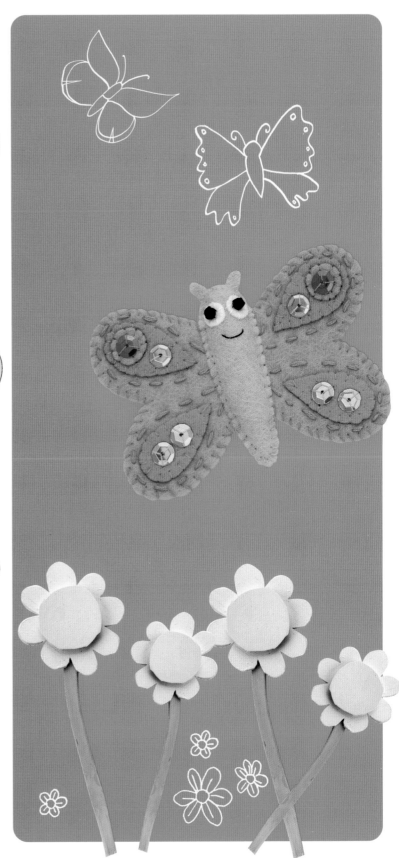

Lucy the Laughing Snail

A friendly snail with a pretty pastel shell. Instead of using embroidery thread to decorate the shell, you could embellish yours with beads or sparkly sequins. You could even use fun printed felt and make a snail with a polka-dot shell or a leopard print one. If we can decorate our houses, then snails can too!

You will need:

Templates and embroidery pattern on page 125

Mint green felt, approx. 2 x 3½in (5 x 9cm)

Fawn (very light brown) felt, approx. 3½ x 4in (9 x 10cm)

Small piece of white felt

Matching sewing threads

Light pink and light turquoise embroidery floss (thread)

2 black seed beads, size 8/0

Tracing paper or parchment paper

Sharp pencil or fine-tipped pen

Polyester stuffing

Needles, scissors, pins

1 Using the templates, cut out two shells from mint green felt, two snails from fawn felt, and two eyes from white felt.

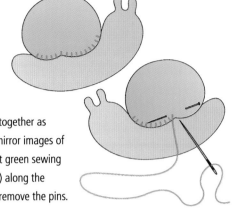

2 Pin the shell and snail pieces together as pictured, so the two snails are mirror images of each other. Using matching mint green sewing thread, whipstitch (see page 10) along the bottom of each shell piece and remove the pins. Set one of the snails aside.

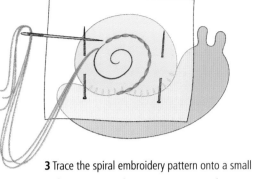

3 Trace the spiral embroidery pattern onto a small piece of tracing or parchment paper using a sharp pencil or fine-tipped pen. Pin the spiral to the center of the felt shell. Cut a length of light turquoise embroidery floss and separate half the strands (so for six-stranded floss, use three strands). Switch to a larger needle if necessary and backstitch (see page 10) a spiral onto the shell, following the line. Remove the pins and carefully tear the paper away from the stitches, using a pin to gently remove any remaining pieces of paper.

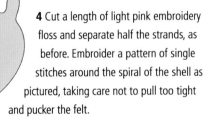

4 Cut a length of light pink embroidery floss and separate half the strands, as before. Embroider a pattern of single stitches around the spiral of the shell as pictured, taking care not to pull too tight and pucker the felt.

5 Sew the eyes in position using whipstitches in white sewing thread. Sew a black seed bead for each pupil with three or four stitches of black sewing thread. Backstitch a smile onto the face using black sewing thread.

6 Hold the front and back snail pieces together, and whipstitch the edges of the snail body together using matching fawn thread. Stuff the body of the snail (see page 11 for tips on stuffing).

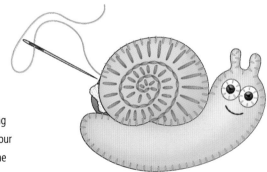

7 Whipstitch around the shell, leaving a hole large enough for your finger, taking care to sew up the gaps where the shell meets the snail's body so no stuffing can escape. Stuff the shell, whipstitch the remaining gap closed, and finish neatly at the back.

Chapter six
At Home

The Dog Family

Woof! Woof! Here's a family of dogs, happily wagging their tails. The dog and puppies are made using honey-colored felt but they'd also look great in brown felt. You can choose to sew the puppies smiling, or with their tongues sticking out. The templates provided are for the puppy with its tail on the right-hand side—to make the other puppy just turn over all the pieces before you start sewing.

You will need:

Templates on page 125

Honey felt, approx. 5¾ x 8in (14.5 x 20cm)

Small pieces of white, black, and pink felt

Matching sewing threads

6 black seed beads, size 8/0

Polyester stuffing

Needle, scissors, pins

The Dog

1 Using the templates, cut out one front body, one back body, one head, two tails, and two ears from honey felt. Cut out two small circles for the eyes from white felt and a small oval for the nose from black felt (see page 9 for tips on cutting out small shapes).

2 Sew the head onto the front body piece using whipstitch (see page 10) in matching honey sewing thread, using the back body shape as a guide to ensure the front and back of the dog will line up neatly when sewn together.

3 Sew the ears to the head using a few whipstitches of matching honey sewing thread, as pictured. Whipstitch the eyes and nose to the face using matching sewing threads, then sew two black seed beads to the eyes for the pupils with three or four stitches of black sewing thread. Backstitch (see page 10) the dog's smile.

4 Whipstitch the two tail pieces together using matching honey sewing thread.

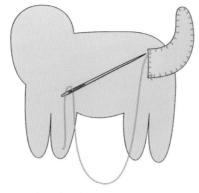

5 Sew the tail to the back body piece using whipstitch in matching honey sewing thread, sewing into the back piece of felt but not through it.

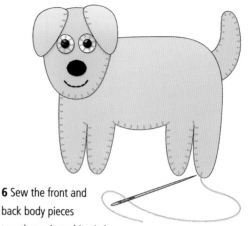

6 Sew the front and back body pieces together using whipstitch in matching honey sewing thread, starting from just below the head and sewing around the legs. Stuff the legs (see page 11 for tips on stuffing).

7 Whipstitch around the dog's body and head, stuffing gradually as you sew until the final gap is closed, turning the dog back and forth as you sew past the tail to ensure the stitches are neat on both sides and folding the ears forward as you sew behind them.

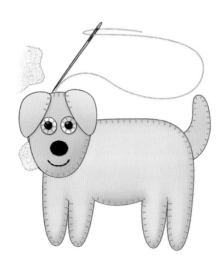

8 If you wish, sew a line of running stitch flush around the edge of the dog's head from bottom to top using honey sewing thread to improve the shape. Carefully sew through all the layers of felt and stuffing to pull the layers closer together. Turn the dog back and forth as you sew to ensure the stitching is neat on both sides and finish neatly at the back.

The Puppies

1 Using the templates, for each puppy cut one front body, one back body, one head, two ears, and two tails from honey felt. Cut out a small oval for the nose from black felt (see page 9 for tips on cutting out small shapes). To make a puppy with its tongue sticking out, also cut out a small tongue shape from pink felt—this should be roughly rectangular but with a curve at one end.

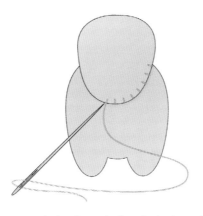

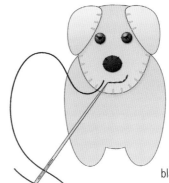

2 Sew the head onto the front body piece using whipstitch (see page 10) in matching honey sewing thread, using the back body shape as a guide to ensure the front and back of the puppy will line up neatly when sewn together.

3 Sew the ears to the head with a few whipstitches in matching honey sewing thread. Whipstitch the nose to the face using black sewing thread and sew two black seed beads for the eyes with three or four stitches of black sewing thread. Backstitch (see page 10) the puppy's smile, as pictured. If you are adding a tongue, sew the center of the smile as a flat line so you can position the straight edge of the tongue flush with the bottom of the smile.

4 If you're adding a tongue, whipstitch the straight edge of the tongue to the mouth using matching pink sewing thread.

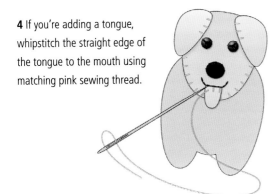

5 Sew the two tail pieces together as in step 4 of the dog instructions. Then sew the tail to the back body piece using whipstitch in matching honey sewing thread, sewing into the back piece of felt but not through it.

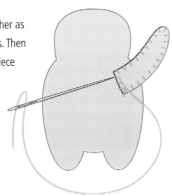

6 Sew the front and back body pieces together using whipstitch in matching honey sewing thread, starting behind one of the ears and sewing down one side of the puppy, around the legs and back up the other side. Stuff the puppy gradually as you sew up the second side (see page 11 for tips on stuffing) until the final gap is closed, folding the ears forward as you sew behind them.

7 If you wish, sew a line of running stitch (see page 10) flush around the bottom edge of the puppy's head using honey sewing thread to improve the shape (as in step 8 of the dog instructions), lifting the tongue (if attached) as you sew behind it and finishing neatly at the back.

Richard the Colorful Rabbit

A happy rabbit, on the hunt for some carrots... I chose lilac felt for my rabbit, which makes him a bit more like the Easter Bunny than a household pet, but a white or brown rabbit would look just as cute! He would make a great Easter gift, and would be a cute (and longer-lasting) alternative to a chocolate egg.

You will need:

Templates on page 126

Lilac felt, approx. 4¼ x 4¾in (10.5 x 12cm)

White felt, approx. 2 x 2in (5 x 5cm)

Small pieces of pale pink, pale lilac, and black felt

Matching sewing threads

Polyester stuffing

Needle, scissors, pins

1 Using the templates, cut out one front body, one back body, and one head from lilac felt, two tails, two eyes, and one tooth piece from white felt, one nose and one of each ear from pale pink felt, and one cheek piece from pale lilac felt. Cut out two small circles for the pupils from black felt (see page 9 for tips on cutting out small shapes).

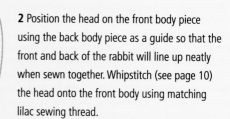

2 Position the head on the front body piece using the back body piece as a guide so that the front and back of the rabbit will line up neatly when sewn together. Whipstitch (see page 10) the head onto the front body using matching lilac sewing thread.

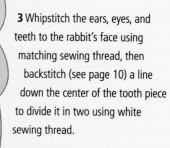

3 Whipstitch the ears, eyes, and teeth to the rabbit's face using matching sewing thread, then backstitch (see page 10) a line down the center of the tooth piece to divide it in two using white sewing thread.

4 Whipstitch the cheeks, nose, and pupils to the face using matching sewing threads, then sew three long stitches onto each cheek using white sewing thread for the whiskers.

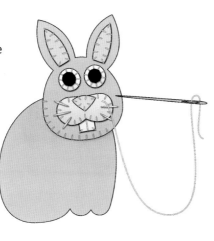

5 Backstitch three lines onto the rabbit's body to mark out the legs, as pictured, using matching lilac sewing thread.

6 Place the two tail pieces together and whipstitch around the edge using white sewing thread, leaving the straight edge unstitched. Stuff the "fluffy" section of the tail but leave the band of felt along the straight edge unstuffed (this will be hidden inside the finished rabbit).

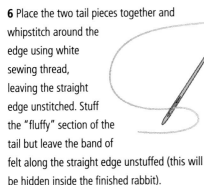

7 Whipstitch the tail to the back body piece using matching lilac sewing thread, sewing into the lilac felt but not through it.

8 Sew the front and back of the rabbit together using whipstitch in matching lilac sewing thread, starting at the right-hand side where the head meets the body. Sew up to and around the head and both ears, stuffing each ear gradually as you sew down the second side (see page 11 for tips on stuffing).

9 Whipstitch down the left side, around the legs, and back up the right side, turning the rabbit back and forth as you sew past the tail to ensure the stitching is neat on both sides. Stuff the head and body gradually as you sew, until the final gap is sewn up.

10 If you wish, sew a line of running stitch (see page 10) flush around the bottom of the rabbit's head, from right to left, using matching lilac sewing thread to improve the shape. Carefully sew through all the layers of felt and stuffing to pull the layers closer together. Turn the rabbit back and forth as you sew to ensure the stitching is neat on both sides, finishing neatly at the back.

Clare the Cuddly Cat

Purr! Purr! This little kitty is sewn from black and white felt but you could make a ginger cat, a brown tabby, or any other color you like. To give your cat markings to match a cat you know, draw around the body and head on a piece of paper and then sketch the markings you'd like to add. Cut the shapes out and use them as templates, adding the felt patches in step 3. You could also add some embroidered stripes.

You will need:

Templates on page 126

Black felt, approx. 3¾ x 7½in (9.5 x 19cm)

Small pieces of white and pink felt

Matching sewing threads

Pink embroidery floss (thread)

Polyester stuffing

Needles, scissors, pins

1 Using the templates, cut out two cats and one head from black felt, two eyes and one of each patch from white felt, and two ears from pink felt. Cut out two small black circles for the pupils, and a small pink triangle for the nose (see page 9 for tips on cutting out small shapes).

2 Place the head onto one of the cat pieces so the ears line up neatly. Pin or hold the layers together and whipstitch (see page 10) the head in position using black sewing thread. Remove the pin, if you've used one.

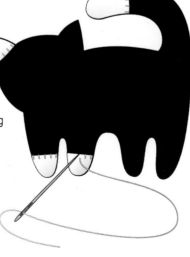

3 Sew on the white patches as pictured using whipstitch in white sewing thread.

4 Whipstitch the eyes and pupils in place using matching sewing threads, and attach the nose and ears with one stitch on each of the triangles' points in matching sewing thread.

5 Cut a length of pink embroidery floss and separate half the strands (so for six-stranded floss, use three strands). Switch to a larger needle if necessary and backstitch (see page 10) the cat's mouth, as pictured. Then add six single stitches in white sewing thread to form the whiskers.

6 Place the front and the back cat pieces together. Starting from the left, where the cat's head meets its body, whipstitch around the edge in black sewing thread. Sew along the legs and up to the bottom of the tail and then stuff the cat's legs (see page 11 for tips on stuffing).

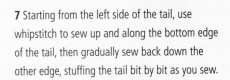

7 Starting from the left side of the tail, use whipstitch to sew up and along the bottom edge of the tail, then gradually sew back down the other edge, stuffing the tail bit by bit as you sew.

8 Whipstitch along the back of the cat and around the head, stuffing the cat gradually until the final gap is sewn shut.

9 If you wish, use black sewing thread to sew a line of running stitch (see page 10) flush around the edge of the cat's head from bottom to top to improve the shape. Carefully sew through all the layers of felt and stuffing to pull the layers closer together. Turn the cat back and forth as you sew to ensure the stitching is neat on both sides, finishing neatly at the back.

Meeow!

Nicola the Naughty Guinea Pig

This furry guinea pig would like to be your friend! Quick to sew and very easy to stuff, this is a great first pet to sew if you're a beginner. If you don't have any ginger felt, simply use brown instead, and you can add white patches to your guinea pig by drawing around the body template and sketching the shapes you'd like to add. Cut these out and use them as templates, and add the white felt patches with whipstitch before beginning step 2.

You will need:

Templates on page 127

Ginger felt, approx. 3¼ x 4½in (8.5 x 11cm)

Small pieces of light brown, white, and black felt

Pink felt, approx. 1¾ x 2in (4.5 x 5cm)

Matching sewing threads

Pink embroidery floss (thread)

Polyester stuffing

Needles, scissors, pins

1 Using the templates, cut out two guinea pigs from ginger felt, one ear from light brown felt, one eye from white felt, and one nose and four feet from pink felt. Cut out a small black circle for the pupil (see page 9 for tips on cutting out small shapes).

Note: This guinea pig has a single layer of felt for each foot, but to make the feet thicker or sturdier cut out eight feet instead of four and sew the two layers together with running stitch (see page 10) or whipstitch (see page 10) in matching pink sewing thread. Or, if you find sewing two small pieces together a bit tricky, use the method for sewing the Owl's feet on page 20, sewing one shape onto a piece of felt and then cutting out the second layer after you've finished stitching.

2 Sew the eye, pupil, and nose onto one of the guinea pig pieces using whipstitch (see page 10) in matching sewing threads. Attach the ear, sewing a line of running stitch (see page 10) around the edge in matching light brown sewing thread.

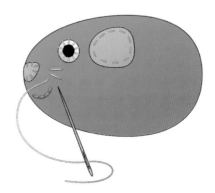

3 Cut a length of pink embroidery floss and separate half the strands (so for six-stranded floss, use three strands). Switch to a larger needle if necessary and backstitch (see page 10) the guinea pig's smile, then use white sewing thread to sew three single stitches for the whiskers.

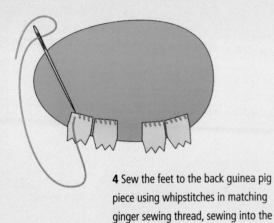

4 Sew the feet to the back guinea pig piece using whipstitches in matching ginger sewing thread, sewing into the back piece of felt but not through it.

5 Sew the front and back of the guinea pig together at the nose using whipstitches in matching pink sewing thread. Whipstitch around the edge of the guinea pig using matching ginger sewing thread, turning the guinea pig back and forth as you sew past the feet to ensure the stitching is neat on both sides. Leave a gap wide enough for your finger, and stuff the body (see page 11 for tips on stuffing). Sew the gap closed, finishing neatly at the back.

Percy the Brilliant Parakeet

A pretty parakeet, looking for somewhere to perch. Parakeets are such colorful birds—why not sew a whole flock in different colors? You could swap the light turquoise felt for a light blue or violet, or change the colors of the whole bird by using yellow for the head and wings and green for the body.

You will need:

Templates on page 127

Light turquoise felt, approx. 4½ x 4½in (11 x 11cm)

White felt, approx. 2½ x 3in (6.5 x 8cm)

Small pieces of yellow, gray, and black felt

Matching sewing threads

Black, gray, and light turquoise embroidery floss (thread)

Polyester stuffing

Needles, scissors, pins

1 Using the templates, cut out two parakeets from light turquoise felt, one wing and one head from white felt, one beak from yellow felt, and one foot piece from gray felt. Cut out a small circle for the eye from black felt (see page 9 for tips on cutting out small shapes).

Note: This parakeet has a single layer of felt for the feet, but to make the feet thicker or sturdier cut out an extra foot piece and sew the two layers together with running stitch (see page 10) or whipstitch (see page 10) in matching gray sewing thread. Or, if you find sewing two small pieces together a bit tricky, use the method for sewing the Owl's feet on page 20, sewing one shape onto a piece of felt and then cutting out the second layer after you've finished stitching.

2 Sew the head onto one of the parakeet pieces using whipstitch (see page 10) in white sewing thread. Pin or hold the wing in place and whipstitch around the top and right-hand edge, as pictured.

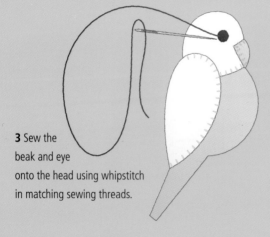

3 Sew the beak and eye onto the head using whipstitch in matching sewing threads.

4 Cut a length of black embroidery floss and separate half the strands (so for six-stranded floss, use three strands). Switch to a larger needle if necessary and backstitch (see page 10) two black lines onto the tail, as pictured. Cut a length of gray embroidery floss and separate half the strands as before. Using the picture as a rough guide embroider a series of curved lines onto the wings, sewing two lines of gray stitching then one line of black, followed by two lines of gray and so on. Either switch between the floss colors as you work down the wing or sew all the gray lines first, leaving a gap between them for filling in the black lines afterward.

5 Sew four very small stitches around the parakeet's neck using black embroidery floss. Cut a length of light turquoise embroidery floss and separate half the strands as before. Sew two stitches along the top of the beak, and three small stitches next to each other to form a small patch on the parakeet's cheek.

6 Cut another length of gray embroidery floss, separate half the strands, and backstitch a series of slightly curved lines onto the parakeet's head, as pictured.

7 Sew the feet onto the back parakeet piece using whipstitch in matching light turquoise sewing thread, sewing into the back piece of felt but not through it.

8 Sew the front and back parakeet pieces together at the beak using whipstitch in matching yellow sewing thread, then sew around the head and along the back of the wing using white sewing thread.

9 Stuff the parakeet's head (see page 11 for tips on stuffing) then whipstitch around the tail and belly using matching light turquoise sewing thread, stuffing gradually as you sew. Turn the parakeet back and forth as you sew past the feet to ensure the stitching is neat on both sides, sew up the final gap, and finish neatly at the back.

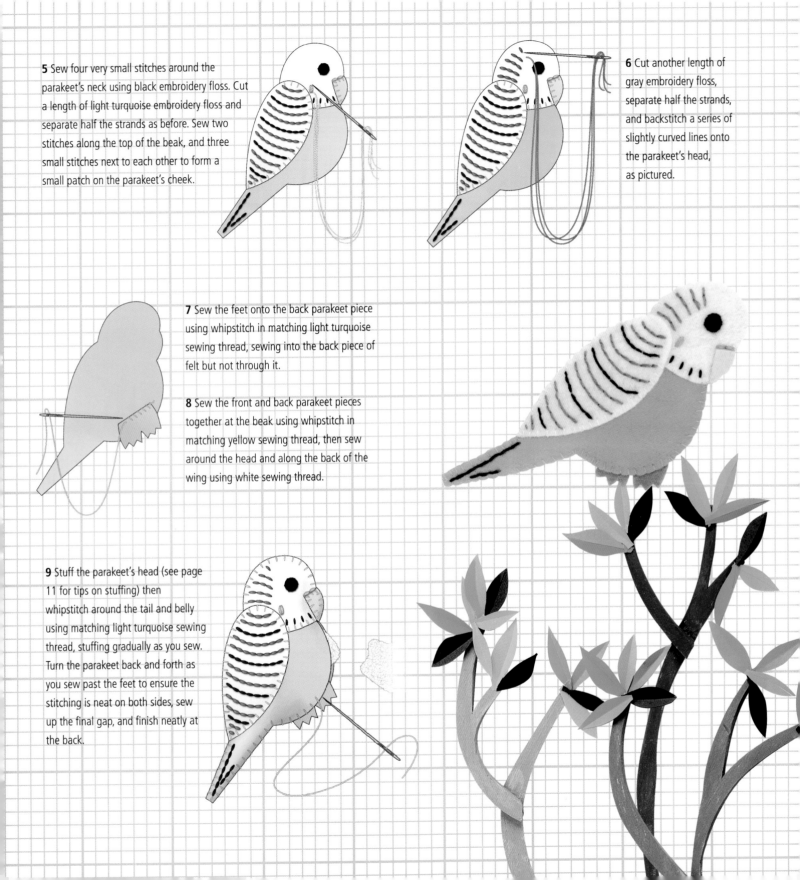

Templates

Fox and cubs page 16

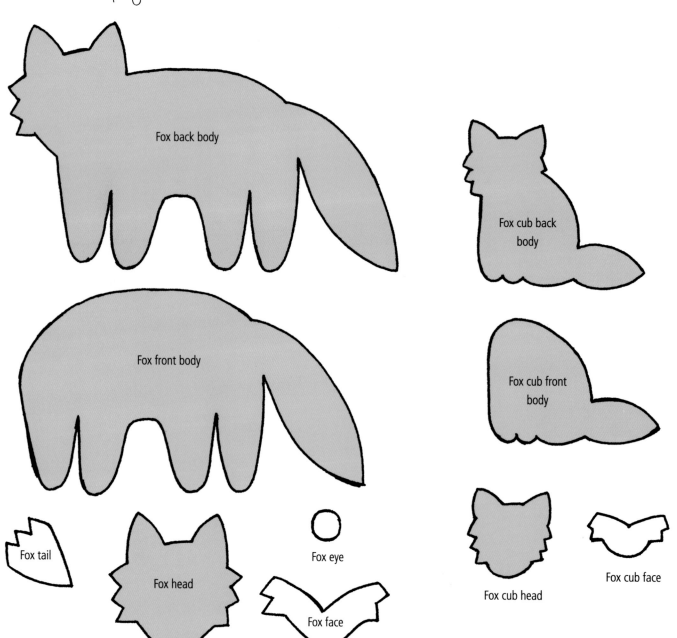

Fox back body

Fox cub back body

Fox front body

Fox cub front body

Fox tail

Fox head

Fox eye

Fox face

Fox cub head

Fox cub face

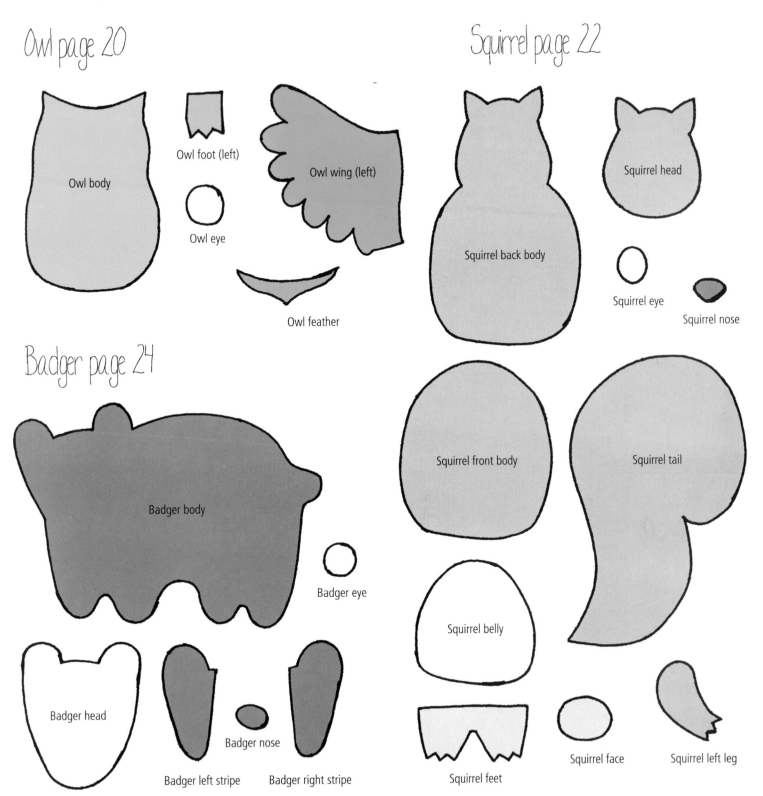

Owl page 20

Owl body

Owl foot (left)

Owl eye

Owl wing (left)

Owl feather

Squirrel page 22

Squirrel head

Squirrel back body

Squirrel eye

Squirrel nose

Squirrel front body

Squirrel tail

Squirrel belly

Badger page 24

Badger body

Badger eye

Badger head

Badger left stripe

Badger nose

Badger right stripe

Squirrel feet

Squirrel face

Squirrel left leg

Deer page 26

Deer tail

Deer head

Deer body (front)

Deer back body

Hedgehog page 28

Hedgehog spikes

Hedgehog eye

Hedgehog

Crocodile page 40

Crocodile

Crocodile eye

Woodland extras page 30

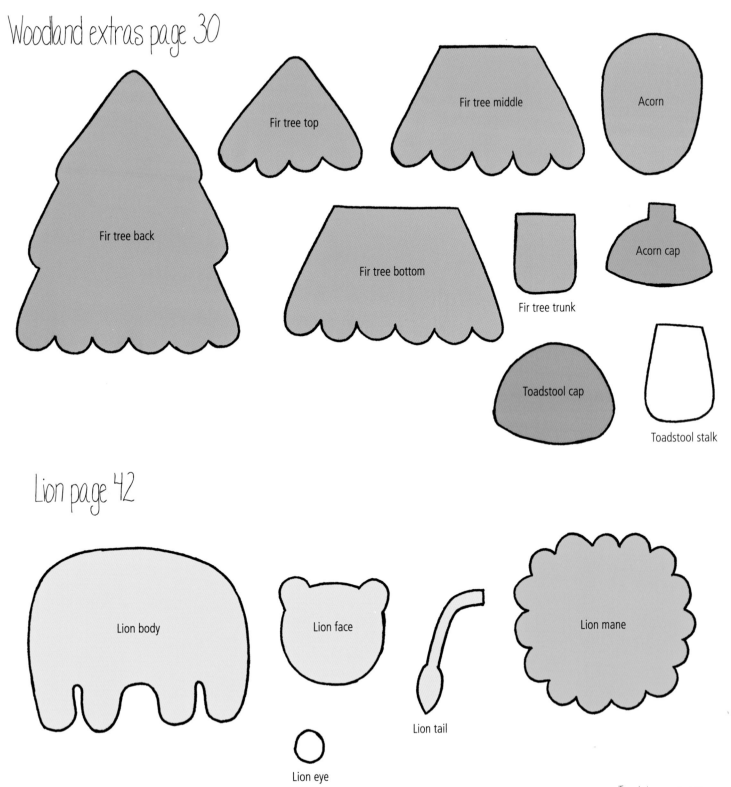

Fir tree top

Fir tree middle

Acorn

Fir tree back

Fir tree bottom

Fir tree trunk

Acorn cap

Toadstool cap

Toadstool stalk

Lion page 42

Lion body

Lion face

Lion tail

Lion mane

Lion eye

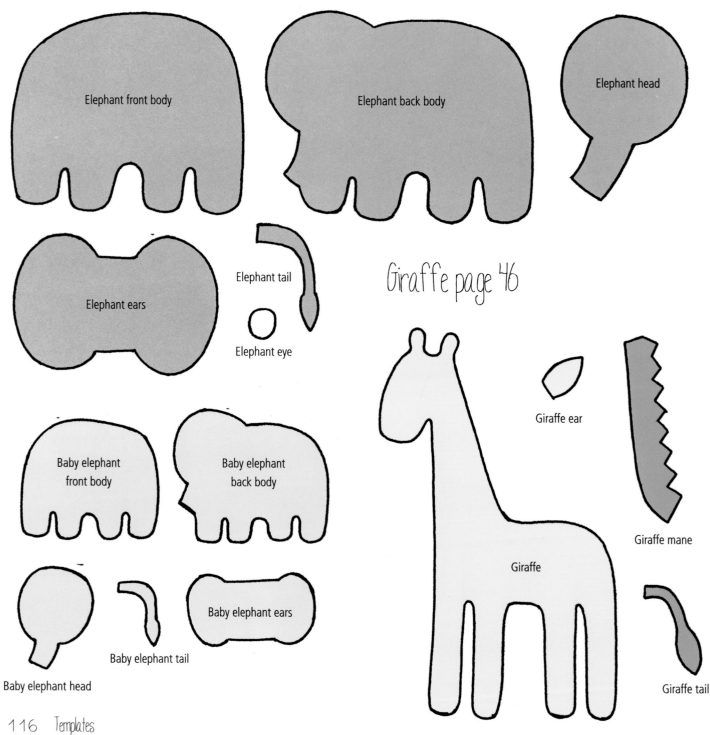

Elephants page 36

Elephant front body

Elephant back body

Elephant head

Elephant ears

Elephant tail

Elephant eye

Giraffe page 46

Baby elephant front body

Baby elephant back body

Giraffe ear

Giraffe mane

Baby elephant head

Baby elephant tail

Baby elephant ears

Giraffe

Giraffe tail

Hippo page 44

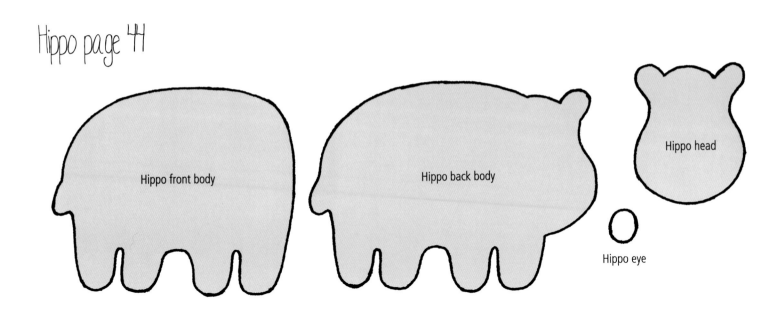

Hippo front body

Hippo back body

Hippo head

Hippo eye

Zebra page 48

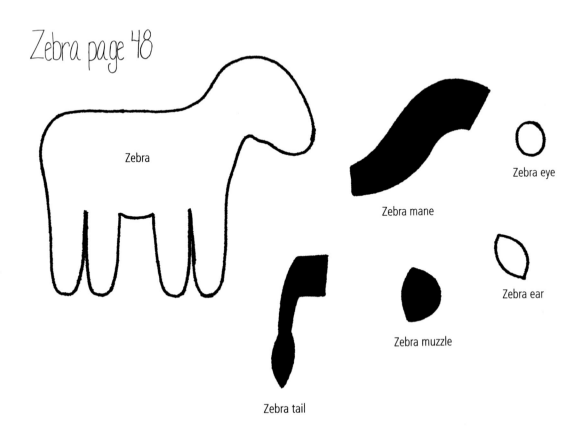

Zebra

Zebra mane

Zebra eye

Zebra tail

Zebra muzzle

Zebra ear

Fish page 52

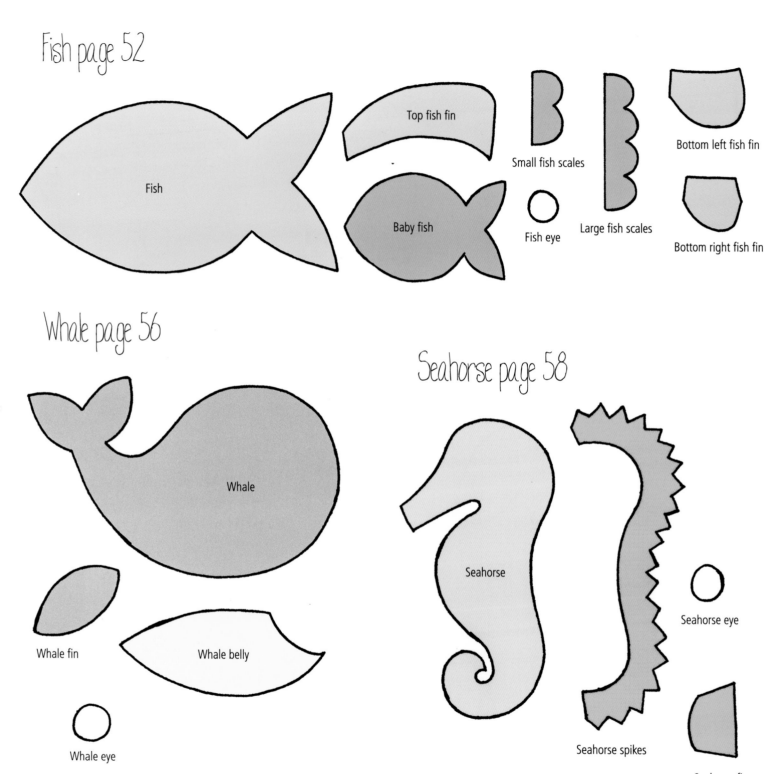

Fish

Top fish fin

Baby fish

Small fish scales

Fish eye

Large fish scales

Bottom left fish fin

Bottom right fish fin

Whale page 56

Whale

Whale fin

Whale belly

Whale eye

Seahorse page 58

Seahorse

Seahorse eye

Seahorse spikes

Seahorse fin

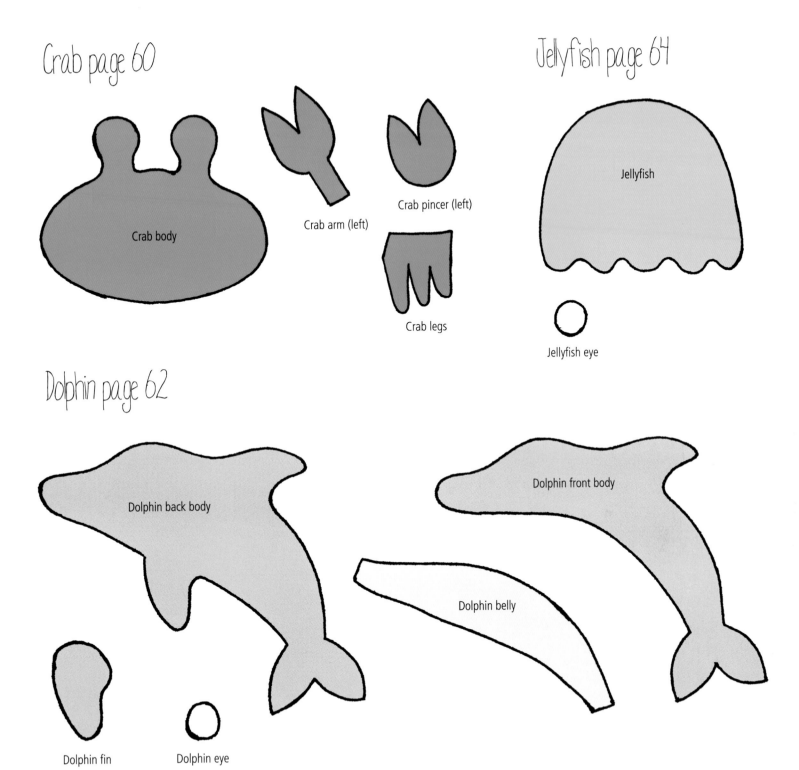

Crab page 60

Crab body

Crab arm (left)

Crab pincer (left)

Crab legs

Jellyfish page 64

Jellyfish

Jellyfish eye

Dolphin page 62

Dolphin back body

Dolphin front body

Dolphin belly

Dolphin fin

Dolphin eye

Chicken and chick page 68

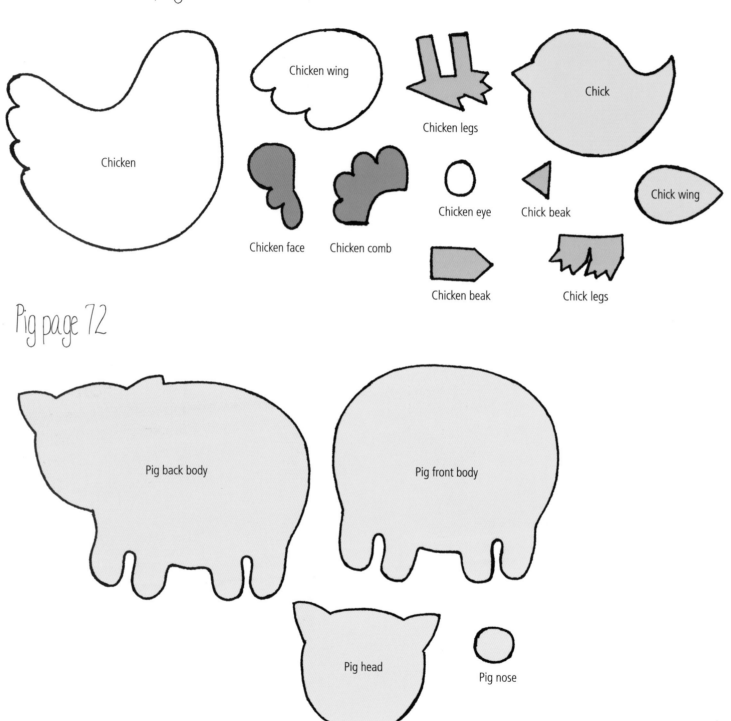

Chicken

Chicken wing

Chicken legs

Chick

Chicken face

Chicken comb

Chicken eye

Chick beak

Chick wing

Chicken beak

Chick legs

Pig page 72

Pig back body

Pig front body

Pig head

Pig nose

Sheep page 74

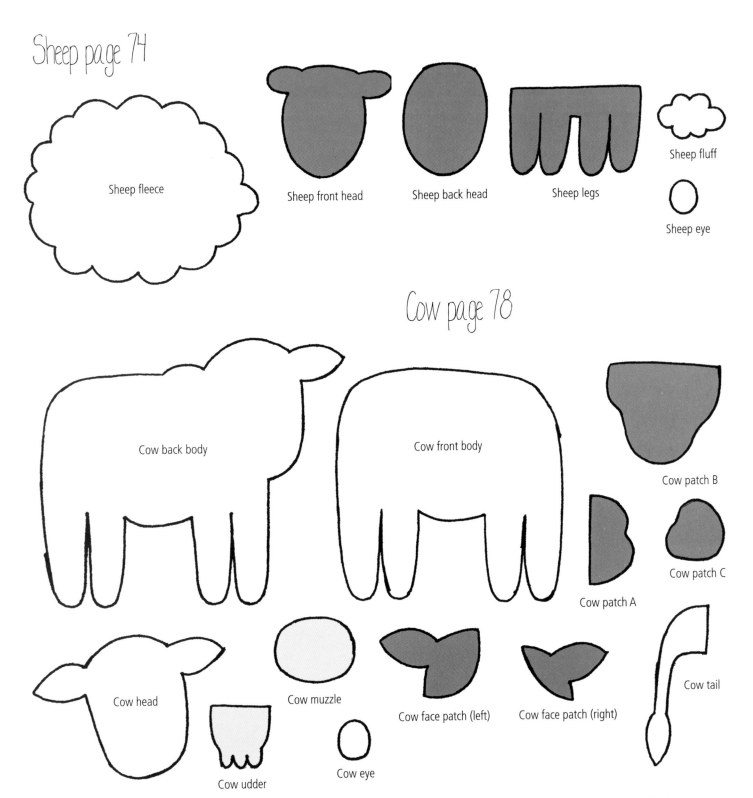

Sheep fleece

Sheep front head

Sheep back head

Sheep legs

Sheep fluff

Sheep eye

Cow page 78

Cow back body

Cow front body

Cow patch B

Cow patch A

Cow patch C

Cow head

Cow muzzle

Cow face patch (left)

Cow face patch (right)

Cow tail

Cow udder

Cow eye

Sheepdog page 76

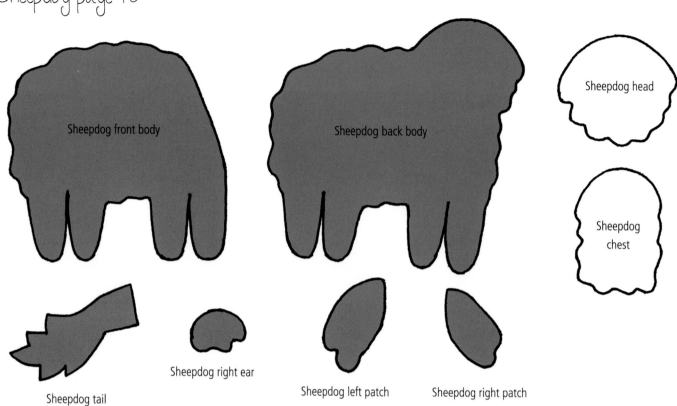

Sheepdog front body

Sheepdog back body

Sheepdog head

Sheepdog chest

Sheepdog tail

Sheepdog right ear

Sheepdog left patch

Sheepdog right patch

Frog page 90

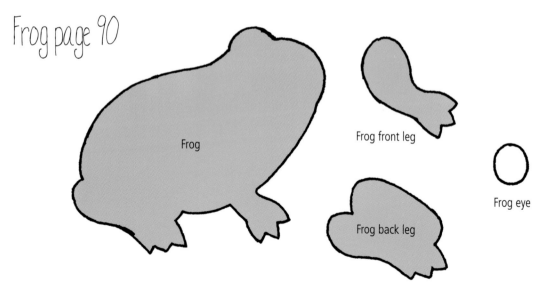

Frog

Frog front leg

Frog back leg

Frog eye

Horse page 82

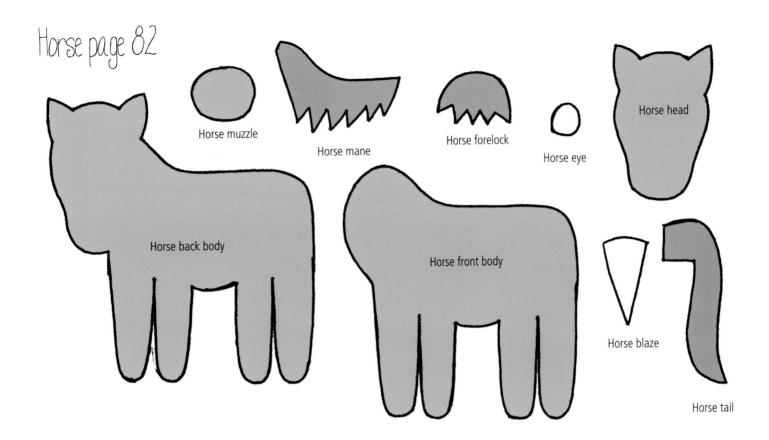

Horse muzzle

Horse mane

Horse forelock

Horse eye

Horse head

Horse back body

Horse front body

Horse blaze

Horse tail

Pigeon page 92

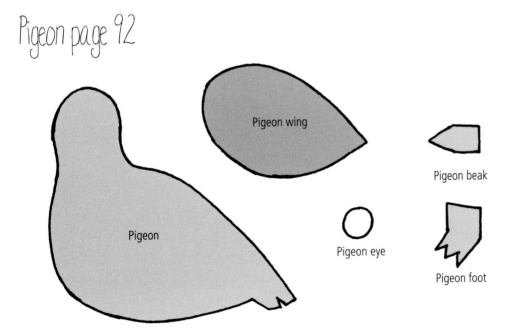

Pigeon wing

Pigeon beak

Pigeon

Pigeon eye

Pigeon foot

Robin family page 86

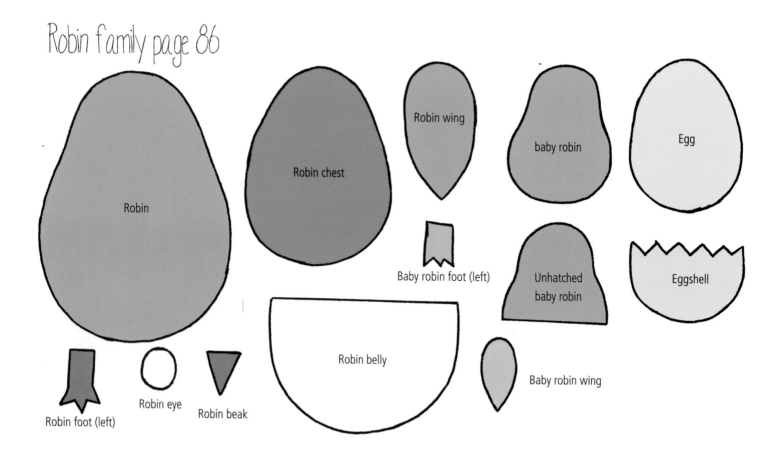

Robin

Robin chest

Robin wing

baby robin

Egg

Baby robin foot (left)

Unhatched baby robin

Eggshell

Robin foot (left)

Robin eye

Robin beak

Robin belly

Baby robin wing

Butterfly page 94

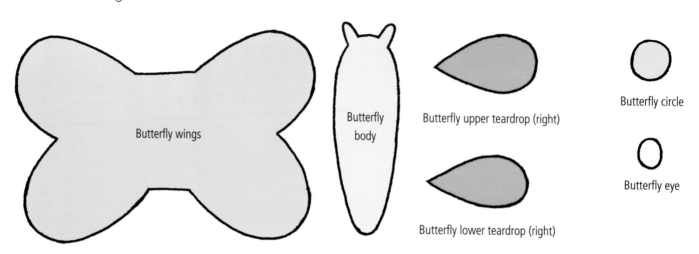

Butterfly wings

Butterfly body

Butterfly upper teardrop (right)

Butterfly circle

Butterfly eye

Butterfly lower teardrop (right)

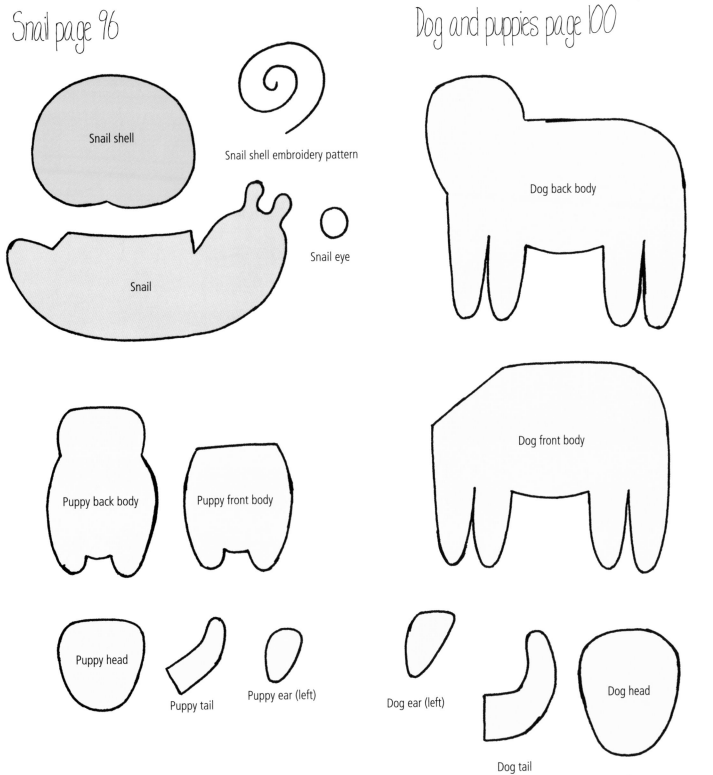

Snail page 96

Snail shell

Snail shell embroidery pattern

Snail

Snail eye

Dog and puppies page 100

Dog back body

Dog front body

Puppy back body

Puppy front body

Puppy head

Puppy tail

Puppy ear (left)

Dog ear (left)

Dog tail

Dog head

Rabbit page 104

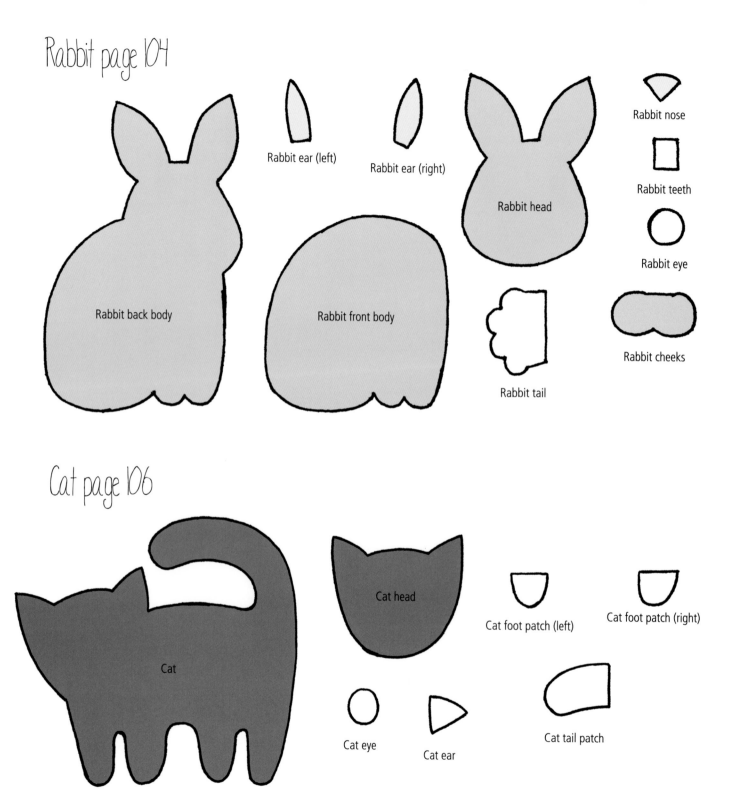

Rabbit ear (left)

Rabbit ear (right)

Rabbit nose

Rabbit teeth

Rabbit head

Rabbit eye

Rabbit back body

Rabbit front body

Rabbit cheeks

Rabbit tail

Cat page 106

Cat head

Cat foot patch (left)

Cat foot patch (right)

Cat

Cat eye

Cat ear

Cat tail patch

Guinea pig page 108

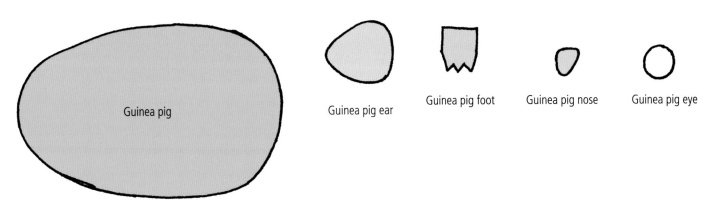

Guinea pig

Guinea pig ear

Guinea pig foot

Guinea pig nose

Guinea pig eye

Parakeet page 110

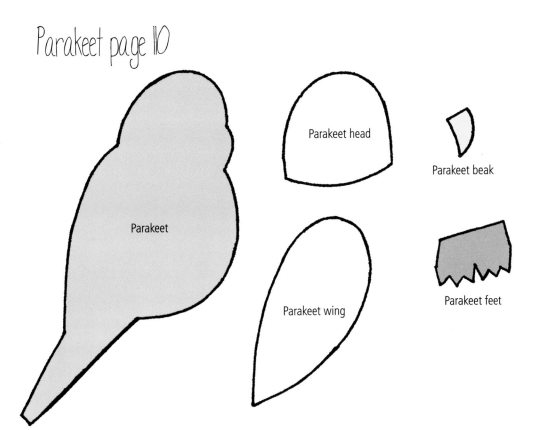

Parakeet

Parakeet head

Parakeet beak

Parakeet wing

Parakeet feet

Suppliers

Index